LANTERN
in the DAWN

Selections
from the Writings of
John E. Zercher

Edited by
E. Morris Sider
and
Paul Hostetler

Evangel Press
Nappanee, Indiana

Introduction

For more than a decade the editorials in the *Evangelical Visitor* attracted the attention of many readers, stimulating discussion, raising questions, and inviting response. The editor's signature, a simple Z, identified an intelligent, probing analysis of current issues in the life and thought of the Brethren in Christ Church (and indeed the church at large) and challenged readers to evaluate their lifestyle and theological presuppositions in the clear light of the scriptures.

John performed his task as "pastor to the denomination" with grace and humility. His perception of issues, and his suggestions for dealing with them, was straightforward and precise. Unfailing devotion to Biblical principles and his church was as strong and visible as his editorial signature.

The challenge to publish selections from his writings emerged spontaneously from various sources—letters to members of the Publication Board, informal conversations, formal requests, and the unanimous agreement in an official board meeting that some desirable memorial be established.

This book, like Caesar's Gaul, is divided into three parts: (1) a brief biography by Dr. E. Morris Sider, (2) editorials with particular focus on the Brethren in Christ, and (3) editorials for a wider readership.

The selections appearing in this volume are in chronological order with the exception of the first one, which serves as an illumination of the title, *Lantern in the Dawn.* Although some parts of the material are slightly abbreviated, the viewpoint of the author is preserved in all cases. Actually, the writings are quoted verbatim, but without the encumberance of repetitious quotation marks.

The authors are well qualified for the task. E. Morris Sider is chairman of the Department of History and Political Science at Messiah College, and the author *Vision for Service, Fire in the Mountains, Nine Portraits, Fruit from Woods and Sands,* and numerous articles in professional journals and periodicals.

Paul Hostetler, for many years secretary of the denominational Publication Board and with extensive pastoral experience, currently serves in the College Advancement Office of Messiah College as Director of Information Services. His previous books include *You're in the Teenage Generation, Perfect Love and War* (editor), and a recent biography of his father entitled *Preacher on Wheels.*

As friends and colleagues of the late John E. Zercher, they share insights and evaluations with balance and objectivity that would escape the more casual observer. We are indebted to them for a "labor of love" in producing this memorial book.

Isaiah B. Harley, Chairman
In behalf of the Publication Board

Table of Contents

LANTERN
in the DAWN

Part 1
Biography
of
John E. Zercher

John Engle Zercher

Quality leadership—creative, selfless, loyal—is a priceless gift to any group of people. John Zercher was such a gift to the Brethren in Christ. He was clearly among those who helped to shape and direct the denomination in the last two decades. The story of his life and an account of his contributions to the brotherhood make an instructive chapter in Brethren in Christ history.

John Zercher was both literally and figuratively cradled in the Brethren in Christ Church. His paternal grandfather, Jacob Zercher of Mount Joy, Pennsylvania, was once a dapper young man; upon conversion, however, he left the world behind and became a very serious Christian, as many Brethren in Christ were in those days. Jacob had literary inclinations: a number of articles and poems from his pen are to be found in the early-twentieth-century issues of the church paper, the *Evangelical Visitor*, which his grandson was to edit years later.

When Jacob's youngest child, Ira, did well in school and determined to obtain a high school education, his father was opposed. He failed to see why his son would need more than an elementary education, and, like many of his fellow church members, he suspected even high school education to be dangerous to the faith. Ira waited until he became of age, and at twenty-one began high school at the Elizabethtown Academy. In the next year, 1910, the Brethren in Christ opened their own school, Messiah Bible School and Missionary Training Home (now Messiah College). Ira was the first student to enroll.

Soon after graduation, Ira married a Kansas farm girl, Anna Gish Engle, a descendant of Jacob Engle, one of the founders of the denomination. Ira and Anna moved to one of her father Ephraim's farms near Abilene, Kansas, to begin their married life, and to take an active role in the Belle Springs church four miles distant, Anna

The following persons gave assistance in the preparation of this biography: Luke Biemesderfer, Mary Ebersole, Ruth Freed, Emerson Frey, Helmut Harder, Henry and Beula Hostetter, Isaiah Harley, Wilmer and Velma Heisey, Mark Hess, Paul Hostetler, Phyllis Lentz, Jay McDermond, Ermon Postels, Donna Soliday, Jon Stepp, Erwin Thomas, Alice Grace Zercher, Charles Zercher, David Zercher, Harold Zercher, Ray Zercher. Special recognition is given to Alice Grace Zercher for preparing tapes and documentary material, and for reading the manuscript.

as Sunday school teacher, Ira as a song leader and Sunday school superintendent. Their home became a favorite place in which to visit, and with good reason: Ira and Anna were warm and friendly people, with a sincere interest in the needs of others, and claimed many relatives and friends, not only in Kansas but spread across the continent as well.

Into this home John was born on August 13, 1916. Surrounded as he and his younger brother Harold were by church and friends and parental love, it is not strange that from his earliest years he should be sensitive to religious values and have a highly developed conscience. As a child he sometimes could not sleep at night because of something he had done during the day. He would then call his parents to his bed to pray for him, and thus be relieved of his trouble.

John attended the local rural one-room schoolhouse. It soon became apparent that he was a bright child. He skipped at least one grade, perhaps two. He outdistanced one teacher in his knowledge of mathematics and found it necessary to instruct her in the subject, which, understandably, did not make John her most popular pupil. He attended high school at Enterprise, riding the more than four miles each way on horseback.

He early developed a passion for books. They were his favorite birthday or Christmas present. He read at noon hours, on Sundays, even during family reunions. He relates in one of his editorials how he frequently read late into the night, becoming too absorbed in his book or magazine to notice that the fire had died out and the room had become cold.

Included in his reading were the denominational papers. John once noted in a letter to a friend that at the age of fourteen he read an article on prophecy in the *Evangelical Visitor*. "It scared the daylights out of me as a lad," he related, "and has made me quite cautious of this type of material ever since." Years later in a letter to another friend, Clarence Boyer, he recalled that his earliest memory of church publications went back to the days when Boyer was editor of the *Sunbeam*, a denominational publication for children: "You had promised to send all who would write a picture of yourself taken by yourself (an incredible feat to a naive Kansas lad of nine or ten). I wrote. I received the picture. Our correspondence has covered a half a century."

With John's reading went thinking—frequent periods of silence when he was obviously absorbing what he had read or seen. He would frequently say to his brother, "Be quiet, I want to think," when they woke up early and Harold wanted to talk. A certain element of seriousness entered even into his play. He and Harold, in normal boyhood fashion, often wrestled with each other. Harold usually won these matches, partly because he eventually became as big as John, partly because John could never take wrestling very seriously, in fact would purposely allow his younger brother to win so he would not hurt his feelings.

These attitudes were compatible with the strong work ethic which prevailed in the Zercher home. The family was always up before daybreak, the father and sons working at their chores by lantern light until the dawn arrived. In recalling with appreciation the attitude toward work which his parents taught him, John wrote in an editorial: "Sometimes there was little money but there was always lots of work. Some of our neighbors would head for town when a rain would halt work in the fields. My father seemed to have more work on a rainy day than a fair one. There were always jobs turning up which my father would put on a rainy-day agenda. This was the time to mend the harness or fix an implement or repair the screen door."

Complementing this work ethic of the family was a strong spiritual emphasis in the home and in the church. Kansas had for a number of years been a seedbed for ideas and activities later adopted throughout the denomination. It was in the vanguard of the Sunday school movement, and had sent all of the first missionaries to Africa and some of the first to India. The Belle Springs church was in the center of these activities. Its pastor, Homer Engle, was progressive in his views, and his wife Myrta, John's first Sunday school teacher, had a college education. Both had a strong and lasting influence on John.

Revival meetings were a part of this religious picture. John was converted at the age of twelve in one conducted by Henry Landis, a passionate evangelist from Des Moines, Iowa. His brother also was converted in the same meeting. Both boys were baptized in Mud Creek on a Sunday afternoon in the following summer.

Hard times came to the Zercher family in the mid-1920's. They left the family farm, briefly rented another piece of land, and then for several years rented a farm from Ray Witter, pastor of a local Brethren in Christ congregation. The coming of the economic depression and the winds of the Dust Bowl, however, compounded a difficult financial situation for the Zerchers. The family barely supported themselves for a while on butchering, but this could not be a long-term solution to their problem. Ira decided to return to Grantham. John remained out of high school following his junior year to prepare for the move.

The decision to move was not based solely on economic considerations; Ira and Anna wanted also to place their sons in the church school at Grantham. The family had retained affectionate ties with Messiah Bible College (as the school in those years was being called). "The highlight of the summer," John wrote later in life, "was the annual Messiah-Upland Alumni picnic at the Abilene city park. I scarcely could wait from one year to the next for this event." John was greatly attracted to the young people who returned from Grantham to Kansas at the end of the school year and around whom his and his friend's social activities centered in the summer months.

Ira had arranged with Messiah Bible College president Enos Hess to manage the Hess farm located adjacent to the school. The family arrived in Grantham in February of 1933, the day before ground was broken for the Alumni Auditorium.

John began his senior year of high school at Messiah Bible College in the fall. He lived at home and between studies helped to farm the land where many of the college buildings now stand. In the next five years he remained out of school two years to work on the farm (following his high school graduation and his college freshman year). He graduated from the junior college in 1938 at the age of twenty-one.

John looked back on his years at Messiah College with considerable pleasure. He was active in extra-curricular functions— writing for the monthly *Clarion*, and taking part in debates, the literary society meetings, and student government. For some time he was also president of the Grantham Church Youth Group. When special attractions elsewhere would result in a small attendance at the group's meeting, the assignment was discouraging for John. Ira insisted that it was John's duty, however, to stay at home to see that the program was carried out. Altogether, a seriousness of purpose appears to have characterized much of John's attitude to studies and school life at Messiah Bible College.

John was determined to complete his college education. Since it was necessary to go elsewhere to do so, he remained out of school after graduation to earn some money. He first sold Christmas cards for John Minter, and then went to Malvern, Ohio, where he worked for two years in a chocolate factory operated by a cousin, Roy Hershey. When that operation collapsed, he returned to Pennsylvania and found employment in a Dairy Herd Improvement Testing program in Lancaster County. John was part of a four-man unit that included three other Brethren in Christ young men—his brother, Clarence Lyons, and Wilmer Heisey. His first significant contacts with Mennonites came in this position, as he moved among them testing their milk on their Lancaster County farms.

While John was still working in this position, World War II broke out. Both he and Harold were drafted into the army. Their action, of course, ran counter to the position taken by the denomination. They claimed in later years that the teaching of the church on nonresistance was not then as clear and as vocal as it became during and after the war. Thus, lacking compelling convictions to remain out, John and Harold entered the army.

Inducted in October, 1941, John took his basic training in Mississippi, and in March, 1942 entered the Army School of Engineering at Fort Belvoir in Virginia. He graduated from the officers' candidate course in June, 1942, and in September, 1943, went overseas, first to London and after D-Day to France and Belgium. As an officer (eventually Captain) in the Corps of Engineers, John issued directives for the construction of roads, hospitals, and port installations, and helped to coordinate administrative and physical work. He took part at no time in combat duty. John separated from the army in May, 1946. A short time later he was appointed a major in the army reserves.

His role in the army, not surprisingly, created problems in his relationship to the church. Many young men in his position were disfellowshipped, as the district officials were permitted to do by action of General Conference. This, however, did not happen to John. The Grantham District, under the leadership of Christian N. Hostetter, Jr., one of the strongest peace advocates in the denomination, believed in a more moderate, redemptive approach, and thus John's name remained on the membership list of the Grantham congregation.

The main problem arose when John returned to the United States and sought to take up church life where he left it. The district decided to place him on probation for a year and a half before full membership privileges would be restored. During this period Hostetter spent much time in counselling John, giving him books to read on nonresistance and persuasively presenting the peace position. Hostetter insisted that John write a confession of error before being allowed to resume full membership privileges. According to his own testimony, John composed a number of statements, none of which were quite satisfactory to Hostetter. In December, 1948, however, John resigned his commission in the army reserves, and soon afterwards wrote a confession that Hostetter considered acceptable. According to the Grantham District Minutes, he was received back into full fellowship with the church in early 1949.

As his editorials clearly show, John became one of the leading peace advocates in the denomination. C. N. Hostetter, Jr. obviously played a leading part in John's change of view; it is difficult, however, precisely to determine what other factors influenced his thinking. Yet despite his adopting of the peace position, John apparently never spoke disparagingly of army life itself. In particular, he had much respect for the discipline that the army taught young men; he thought he knew persons in civilian life who could benefit by such discipline. He also retained a sense of patriotism. Although he strongly objected to the Christian flag and the stars and stripes being flown together, he respected the national flag and did not hesitate to salute it when the occasion seemed appropriate.

On returning from Europe, John continued his education by enrolling at Franklin and Marshall College in Lancaster. Here he majored in business administration and paid his way by using GI grants and waiting on tables in the college dining room. He was a president of the campus Business Club and an active member of the Goethean Literary Society. In June, 1947 he graduated magna cum laude.

Several months before graduation, John accepted a position as assistant to the business manager at Millersville State College. Here for the first time in his life he earned a comfortable salary. His lifestyle reflected the change—an interesting development for one from an economically poor background. He began to eat in good restaurants and decorated his apartment on campus in great style, buying good furniture and persuading a cousin, Mary Eshelman, to make the drapes. His natural inclination towards good order, probably strengthened by army life, showed in the great pride he took in the tidiness of his apartment. He liked to boast that he could open his bedroom drawers and find his clothes in the dark.

During these post-war years, John frequently attended non-Brethren in Christ churches, including a Presbyterian church in Lancaster. He was obviously attracted by the more sophisticated services he found outside his own denomination at the same time that he was wrestling with its peace position. That he was not lost to the Brethren in Christ is at least in part owing to the fact that in the summer of 1948 he began to date Alice Grace Hostetter, daughter of Henry and Beula Hostetter and niece to C. N. Hostetter, Jr. At that time John was president of the area Messiah College alumni chapter. He arranged his first date with Alice Grace by placing her on the food committee for an alumni picnic and then driving her to the committee meeting. They were married in the summer of 1950.

By this time he had spent a year at Princeton Theological Seminary. It is not clear why he chose to go to seminary and into the ministry rather than to follow a business career. Later in life he spoke of the ministry as having offered a suitable challenge to him. And he sometimes told of meeting Mrs. Graybill Wolgemuth one day in Lancaster and being challenged by her observation that no one in his father's family had gone into the ministry of the church. Having considered several seminaries, John had chosen Princeton because of its reputation for scholarship. He quickly discovered, however, how much a school boy he was in this citadel of learning. He used to say that on arriving at Princeton and not fully understanding the meaning of such elementary terms as the incarnation, he found himself at first asking foolish questions and giving simple answers.

Princeton challenged John's thinking. Among his favorite courses was one on pastoring, and another taught by the famed Andrew Blackwood. He was excited about theology and absorbed such words and concepts then being discussed as *koinonia*, cell groups, and the Philips translation. In his first two years he enjoyed traveling with gospel teams to assist ministers and to work with youth groups. In his last year he occasionally filled pulpits for absent ministers. The visits of church leaders, among them C. N. Hostetter, Jr., provided John opportunities to discuss questions about the church with which he wrestled.

On his graduation from seminary in 1952, John accepted the pastorate at Pequea in Lancaster County. Pequea was probably one of the few congregations in the denomination at that time which would have found acceptable a pastor with both a seminary (particularly Princeton) and a military background. On the other hand, the congregation at first offered no salary and no parsonage. It was, moreover, a small and somewhat discouraged band of members. In a number of ways Pequea was different from the kind of congregation John's fellow seminarians had expected to obtain.

To support his growing family (eventually the Zerchers had five sons—Gene, Richard, Daryl, Charles, and David), John returned to Millersville State College, again to work in the business office. He was eventually given charge of student services. Without expertise in the area, John converted an old gymnasium and a primitive bookstore into a student center, containing a refreshment and recreational area, and a bookstore planned and operated along the lines of the most recent merchandising practices. It was the first of its kind in the Pennsylvania state college system. In time, Pequea gave John a half-time salary, which enabled him to reduce his work at the college to a part-time basis.

John pastored the Pequea congregation from 1952 to 1958. He did much visiting, making deliberate attempts to reach out to the non-Brethren in Christ elements in the community, and he organized his small congregation to follow his example. He began a remodeling program for the building, introduced summer Bible schools, brought in special speakers, organized family life conferences, and arranged for special social occasions, such as "sip and sing" events for the young people and refreshments after some meetings. To facilitate serving refreshments, John bought a punch bowl as a wedding anniversary gift for Alice Grace. The bowl matched glasses given to them as a wedding present. The Zerchers took the set to church to use on social occasions.

Although not a fluent speaker, John gave his congregation thought-provoking messages. He began his ministry determined to preach sermons which would hold a high standard before the congregation. This approach was modified when he discovered that one of his parishioners remained in bed on Saturday in order to have sufficient strength to attend church on Sunday and that another member had suffered a large financial loss in his farming. He was then convinced that sermons of comfort and encouragement were also needed. These two levels of ministry were later to be reflected in his editorials. John also taught his congregation to appreciate the great hymns of the church in addition to the gospel songs they had always enjoyed.

By the time John left Pequea in 1958 he had in many respects turned the congregation around. It had grown some in numbers, and, what was more important, had ceased to be an inward-looking group of believers. John had helped to set the stage for the later development of the congregation.

John looked back with considerable fondness on this period of his life. Some of his editorials touch on the work of the pastor. "The pastor," he wrote in one of them, "who by love and a selfless ministry has won the devotion of his people and the respect of the community has a rewarding life that is unsurpassed." Without intention on his part, that expression may be taken as a picture of John's own ministry at Pequea.

John's wider denominational activities had begun in 1952 with his appointment to the Publication Board. This appointment was the beginning of a relationship with Evangel Press that was to last the rest of his life.

In 1958, when Erwin Thomas resigned as manager of Evangel Press to accept a pastorate, John was appointed to succeed him. His managerial experience and acquaintance with Evangel Press as Publication Board member made him a logical choice. The family moved to Indiana in October, 1958, living first in the onage of the Union Grove Church and then, in April, 1960, moving into a house which they had built near Nappanee.

As manager, John directed both the wholesale and publishing departments of Evangel Press. His work took him to numerous meetings and conventions to display the products of the press. He also traveled to merchandise displays to choose trinkets on which to print scripture verses. He did not greatly enjoy this phase of his work, since he was not certain that the church should promote spending money on such items, nor did he think that sanctifying trinkets with Bible verses did much to benefit the cause of Christ.

He enjoyed more his work as a publishing agent, a role that John largely conceptualized and developed. In this role, he bore a large measure of responsibility for two important publications of the early 1960's—the *Minister's Manual* (1960 edition) and the new church hymnal (released in 1963). John not only saw the manual through the press but also did much of the writing. His concern for a dignified and thoughtful approach to church worship may be seen in the place given in the manual to public prayers (a departure from the earlier edition) and to a fuller form of ritual.

The new church hymnal reflects, among other interests, John's appreciation for the great hymns of the church and for meaningful and effective responsive readings. John helped to compile these readings; he worked on the principle that such readings should have parallel thoughts and contain a dramatic quality. It was John, of course, who as publishing agent obtained copyrights, and supervised the making of the plates and the preparation of indexes. One of the tunes in the hymnal ("Jesus, Friend of Little Children") was named for his son Daryl who was killed by a car in front of his home in April, 1962, during John's work on the book.

One of John's major contributions to Evangel Press in these years was his insistence on changing from letter press to offset printing. The change, made shortly after his tenure as manager ended, enabled the press to offer a wider range of printing services.

In his efforts to make Evangel Press a more profitable enterprise, John experienced considerable frustration. He began each new year with hope, but the audit at the end seldom vindicated that hope. Audit time produced in John the few visibly depressed moments of his life.

In 1967, John Hostetter, then editor of the *Evangelical Visitor*, left that office for the bishopric. John was appointed by the Publication Board to take his place. He accepted because he could more directly use his seminary training and pastoral experience in the new position. He considered the editor to be, in a sense, the pastor to the denomination. He liked also the challenge of writing and handling articles. In fact, already as a boy he had dreamed of some day helping to edit and publish books and journals. That dream, which he had thought impossible of fulfillment, had now come true.

As editor, John made some changes in the *Evangelical Visitor*, although none of them were of a radical nature. The change to offset printing meant that John had greater flexibility in the use of color and types of paper, which he used to advantage. He introduced a letter-to-the-editor column, and did not hesitate to print controversial articles; the stimulation from both, he thought, would be good for the readership. He began a "Between Brethren" section (usually carried on the back cover) on issues of particular concern to the Brethren in Christ community.

John's editorial policies are clear. He attempted to maintain a balance between doctrinal and devotional articles. He tried to include material that reflected the various elements of the church's heritage, but he was hampered in carrying out this policy by an abundance of writing on Anabaptist subjects but a scarcity on Wesleyan and Pietist ones. Although he encouraged Brethren in Christ authors to contribute to the paper, he seems not to have insisted as much as he could have done, perhaps because he considered that those who could write well or had important ideas to discuss seemed already too busy to publish in the *Evangelical Visitor*. He used some reprints, often from Mennonite sources.

John's editorials quickly became the most distinctive feature of the new *Evangelical Visitor*. Many persons have observed that the editorial was the first item they read on receiving the current issue. The editorials will undoubtedly stand as one of his major contributions to the Brethren in Christ Church.

They are wide ranging, no subject of concern to the denomination remaining untreated. The editorials show that John not only recognized the important issues but had also an accurate sense for the denomination's position on them. He was judicious in handling such subjects. Although not always agreeing with the church's position, he did not allow his own opinions and sympathies to prevent him from understanding and relating points of view which he did not hold with great enthusiasm.

His editorials were seldom the product of quick and careless thinking. On the contrary, they were often the sounding board for ideas that he had long turned over in his mind or had discussed with friends or fellow churchmen. They sometimes had their origin in what he observed. One editorial was written after he had attended a meeting in which he learned that some leaders in the denomination were admitting into church membership persons who had not sufficiently broken with their sinful past. He wrote another one against displaying the national flag with the Christian flag following a conversation with a young friend who had observed the frequency with which the two were being flown together in the Brethren in Christ churches.

Writing was not particularly easy for John. He admitted confusion about the proper use of commas and other forms of punctuation. Because of a crowded schedule, he frequently wrote against a fast-approaching deadline, which could not have done much to improve his style. He sometimes gave his editorials to others to read before printing, but it does not appear that he did so consistently. But what he lacked in style he made up in strength of thought, with the result that the reader comes away from the editorials with a clear understanding of their meaning and impressed by their message.

As editor, John carried on a large correspondence with his readers. Not surprisingly, some of the letters he received were critical, sometimes of his editorials. John took criticism well. He did not always reply to a sharply worded letter, but when he did so he was invariably conciliatory. One reader objected to an article in which a photograph of hippies and another of a drunk were shown. John explained that Christians should see the ugly as well as the nice side of life. In one reply he conceded that perhaps the article should not have been published, but he does not appear greatly to regret having done so.

There were letters of another kind as well. One elderly woman wrote that she wanted to continue her subscription but she was now in a retirement home and had only $8.00 a month for spending money. John answered that the office staff was moved by her letter and had decided to pay for her subscription. He also solicited funds from *Evangelical Visitor* readers to finance the air-mail sending of the paper to missionaries.

As denominational editor, John's work went beyond producing the *Evangelical Visitor*. He was general editor of the Heritage Series, and assumed editorial responsibilities for such books as *On Being Brethren in Christ* (designed for prospective church members) and Carlton O. Wittlinger's, *Quest for Piety and Obedience: The Story of the Brethren in Christ.*

In the last twenty years of his life, John became involved in the work of the denomination far beyond his assignments at Evangel Press and as denominational editor. Crucial to this broader work was his appointment in 1960 to the Board of Administration as United States Treasurer and by virtue of that office to the Board of Directors. This position he held until 1974. In this role, John came into close working relationship with the denomination's leaders.

These leaders came to recognize John's abilities and commitment, and thus they trusted him with increasing responsibilities. John responded to this trust and challenge and developed into one of the denomination's most effective churchmen in recent years.

As United States Treasurer, John received no remuneration for a work which took a considerable amount of his spare time. The Board once proposed to pay him $400 a year for his efforts, but he refused the offer. He explained to his wife that he often could not find $400 to pay the church's bills; where, then, could he find that much money to pay himself? In fact, when on occasion the denominational treasury was empty and bills needed to be paid, John drew from his own very modest bank account to cover the amount until the needed money arrived.

From 1967 to his death John served on the Board for Schools and Colleges, for all of those years as its chairman. Even earlier, beginning in 1959, he had become a member of the Trustee Board of Messiah College. He served also in this office until his death, in his later years as secretary of the board and as chairman of the board's Academic and Faculty Affairs Committee. He became a member of the Board of Trustees of Niagara Christian College in 1969.

John was a strong supporter of the denomination's schools. All of his sons attended Messiah College, and he printed everything that the college news office sent him for the *Evangelical Visitor.* He was the leading voice in the United States urging his fellow American churchmen to come to the aid of Niagara Christian College in its rebuilding program following the destruction by fire of its auditorium-gymnasium in 1971.

He saw himself as a mediator between the schools and the denomination. He encouraged the colleges to make special efforts to hear and work with the church; he told the denomination that it should not expect more of its educational institutions than it did of its congregations and families.

One of John's many creative ideas, first enunciated by him in 1970, was a foundation to protect the financial integrity of the denomination and its institutions and to encourage their growth. What resulted after much discussion and persuasion on the part of John and others was the Jacob Engle Foundation. He was actively associated with the Foundation from its beginning in 1972 as a member of the Board of Directors.

From his Princeton and Pequea days, John had retained a keen interest in seminaries and seminarians. He promoted the training of pastors in seminaries rather than in Bible schools or in fifth-year college programs. Ministers with seminary training, he insisted, could better serve the increasingly better educated and professional membership of the church. His interest in seminarians came in part from his view of them as future church leaders; he was concerned that as future leaders they understand the doctrines of the Christian church in general and of the Brethren in Christ in particular. His concern was all the greater because the young men in the denomination were being trained in a variety of seminaries and Bible schools, none of them Brethren in Christ.

These concerns found expression in the Committee for Ministerial Training on which he served from its creation in 1972. Out of this context he took the lead in conducting retreats for seminarians. Held every two years, these retreats have brought together most students currently in seminary for several days of intensive lectures and discussion on the church and its doctrines. John did much of the planning, soliciting of funds, and correspondence for these retreats. It was a labor of love. As one participant has put it, John treated seminarians as his sole possession. His interest was a reflection of that shown to him by church leaders in his own seminary days.

In his last few years, John was much involved in the development of the Foundation Series, a Sunday school curriculum planned jointly by the Brethren in Christ, the Church of the Brethren, and several Mennonite groups. Over the years, the Brethren in Christ had explored similar cooperative efforts with other churches, but John and his colleagues were not convinced that there was enough flexibility in the other groups or sufficient common understanding among them to make the venture successful from a Brethren in Christ point of view. It was different, John maintained, with groups from an Anabaptist background. He observed in them a greater willingness to dialogue and to search for common ground.

John's was the major Brethren in Christ voice in the exploratory talks and later development of the Foundation Series. He made it clear to the other church groups that terminology acceptable to the Brethren in Christ would need to be used in the printed materials; the curriculum must reflect what all of them had in common. But John went beyond this to promote such Brethren in Christ views as the work of the Holy Spirit and encouraged his Mennonite and Church of the Brethren colleagues to challenge their readership with such teaching.

To promote the Foundation Series in the denomination, John traveled some 10,000 miles during several weeks in 1977. His last assignment, cut short by his death, was to serve as the Brethren in Christ editor of the Youth/Adult part of the Series curriculum.

In 1973 John and Alice Grace traveled to Africa to participate in the celebrations of the seventy-fifth anniversary of Brethren in Christ mission work in Zambia and Rhodesia (now Zimbabwe). John came back with a great respect for the church in Africa. He insisted that the church in foreign countries must be treated with integrity and be made to feel equal with the church in North America.

From the experiences of this trip came his vision for an international fellowship of the Brethren in Christ. His proposal to the denomination's Men's Fellowship for funding an international conference of Brethren in Christ leaders led to discussion with the Board for Missions and eventually to an international fellowship meeting following General Conference in 1978. In turn John was excited by the new contacts and the new world that was opening to him because of the conference. He presented the historic and doctrinal background of the church to the international delegates and served on the Findings Committee.

He enjoyed attending General Conference. On the floor, he spoke frankly yet thoughtfully; he sponsored issues with conviction and usually with success. In 1971 he preached the conference sermon, "Let the Wind Blow." Because he could incorporate meaningful content into attractive forms, he frequently had program responsibilities. Thus for the church's two-hundredth anniversary celebrations at General Conference in 1978, John served as a member of the program committee, acted as chairman of the advisory committee for the writing and production of the pageant *Pilgrimage* (written by Norman Bert), and wrote the responsive readings for the centennial ceremonies surrounding the conference sermon.

John moved widely in other church circles. For a number of years he was treasurer of the Christian Holiness Association. He attended conventions of the National Association of Evangelicals. For the Brethren in Christ displays at the meetings of these organizations, John developed the symbols of the cross, towel and basin, which, with the additional figure of the dove, later became essentially the official emblem of the denomination.

John enjoyed being with Mennonites; he appreciated them for their challenge to his thinking as well as for their openness to his ideas. Among his favorite friends were those in the Meeting House, a group of Mennonite editors who met periodically for fellowship and exchange of ideas. He was one with his Mennonite friends and others in regretting what he considered the sometimes too nationalistic stance of the NAE and the CHA, and he was dismayed by NAE resolutions in support of capital punishment.

As active as John was in the denomination, he also shared in the

life of his home congregation at Nappanee—a reflection of his
conviction that the congregation is "where the rubber meets the
road," as he sometimes expressed the thought. He regularly
attended all the meetings of the congregation, including prayer
meetings, and would try to arrange his board and committee
meetings in such a way as to arrive home in time for the services.
He held a wide range of congregational offices over the nearly
twenty years of his membership in the church—Sunday school
teacher, Sunday school superintendent, church board member,
church treasurer, and others.

His work on the congregation's Commission on Fellowship and
Ministries, which he chaired from 1970 to 1977, appears to have
been especially meaningful to him. The commission conducts
fellowship activities for the congregation, ministers to the sick,
and welcomes visitors to the services. John took the lead in such
activities. His home was one of those in the congregation which
frequently entertained guests who had come to the church.

Almost incredibly John found time to serve in the community.
He occasionally preached in the local churches, most frequently in
the Presbyterian. He was a member of the local Kiwanis Club and
its president in 1971-1972 (the year in which the club celebrated its
golden anniversary, thus requiring more than the usual amount of
work from its president). In his last years, John wrote the club's
weekly bulletin, the *Kiwanibull*, which under his editorship one
year received the national award for the best bulletin for a club of
its size. In 1978 he persuaded the club to observe a sacrificial meal
during Thanksgiving and to give the amount saved to a local relief
agency. John was chosen to be chairman of the committee in
charge of Nappanee's centennial celebrations in 1974, in part
because of his ability to moderate differing views on the ways in
which to celebrate. John himself considered it appropriate to
celebrate by growing a beard.

As his children entered school, John became involved in other
local activities. He revived a faltering PTA by serving one year as
its president. His older sons belonged to the 4H Club, so he sat on
the local committee and served one year as its president.

John had a quiet yet effective way of speaking to local issues. He
commended the area's school superintendent for hiring a black
person as a teacher. He wrote to the local bowling alley proprietor,
protesting that if the proprietor installed a bar and lounge he
could not recommend that his sons patronize the place. He sent
letters to his senators and congressman in Washington, once to
thank one of them for voting against a military appropriations
bill, another for voting for a volunteer rather than a drafted army.

There remained his family. He made as much time for them as possible, trying to fit his work around their schedules, not always with success. On one occasion, because he could not attend the school musical in which one of his sons played, he sat through the rehearsal. In his last year he bought an outdoor grill; he enjoyed doing a family cook-out, dressed in the denim chef's cap and apron that his daughter-in-law had made him.

He taught his sons the discipline of work, as he himself had been taught in his earlier years, although this frequently meant helping to deliver their newspapers in bad weather and hauling the family lawn mower or vacuum cleaner in the car to jobs the sons had undertaken. When Alice Grace returned to teaching, John joined the sons in doing the housework and assumed the sole responsibility for making breakfast.

Only occasionally did he find time for an extended family holiday. When he did, the trips were connected with some church activity, such as traveling to General Conference. As his sons grew older, he occasionally took the family to a professional baseball game in Chicago, switching his allegiance from the St. Louis Cardinals to the Chicago White Sox to fit the situation.

Outside his family and his work in the church, his great love was gardening. As soon as the seed catalogues began to arrive in the early months of the year, John would be convinced that spring was just around the corner. Like most gardeners, he usually planted more than the family could consume; friends and neighbors were thus recipients of his agricultural generosity. He took a farmer's delight in strolling to the garden before entering the house for lunch or dinner to see how well the garden had done since he last saw it.

The work ethic to which he had been born clearly remained a strong one for John. Even his most enjoyable recreation, gardening, was a form of work. He owned a set of golf clubs given to him by friends, but he seldom used them; he insisted that he wanted to do something productive in his spare moments and his garden fulfilled that requirement. Holidays were combined with church work, as on the family's camping trip to General Conference in 1965 during which he did pressing office work while his family relaxed and played.

John took additional assignments because it was difficult for him to say no to a new challenge. If he did give up one position he soon filled the empty space with another. He clearly carried too heavy a load, one result being that he sometimes fell behind schedule in completing assignments and producing the *Evangelical Visitor*.

Although he drove himself hard, John was a congenial man
with his staff and colleagues at Evangel Press. His sense of humor,
quick smile, open office door, frequent humming of tunes, and
usual inquiry about members of the family made him appear as
much friend as employer and church leader. Removing his glasses
and nibbling at their ends while talking did nothing to destroy this
image.

John possessed a first-rate mind, undoubtedly never pushed to
its full potential. His personal library suggests the depth and
range of his reading—it contained books by Emil Brunner, Karl
Barth, Reinhold Niebuhr, Soren Kierkegaard, Elton Trueblood,
Will Durant, and Winston Churchill. Two of the books he had
much underlined were *A Man in Christ* by James Stewart and *The
Cost of Discipleship* by Dietrich Bonhoeffer.

John was not unaware of his abilities. He accepted so many
assignments because he knew he was big enough for them. But he
retained a good sense of proportion about himself, not taking
himself too seriously and enjoying a good joke at his own expense.
He used his good mind not to fight battles and win arguments but
to find his way through problems without creating antagonisms.
He could undoubtedly have commanded a high income elsewhere;
instead he chose to remain with the church and the press at a very
modest salary.

These qualities make it easier to comprehend John's difficulty
in understanding or appreciating flashy evangelists and television
personalities and his repeated suggestions in the editorials that the
Brethren in Christ would serve the cause of Christ better, generally
speaking, if they gave their money to their own denomination. His
own style was undemonstrative; he once observed that his meaningful religious experiences were private ones. He was moved by
prayer—public prayers especially. The high point in a church
service, John considered, was the moment when a pastor brought
his congregation before God. The verbal hesitancy that sometimes
marked his speech seemed to disappear when he himself performed this role.

On the week of his birthday and a few days before his death, he
talked at length with his pastor. John remarked that the past year
had been a good one for him. He was concerned about his unusu-
ally heavy schedule and was frustrated that he had not been able to
locate an office assistant. He noted that in two years he would be
retiring. In his retirement he was thinking of taking some courses
in theology, probably at the Associated Mennonite Biblical Seminaries in Elkhart. He also planned to do some writing, including a
book on nonresistance and completing one for the Heritage Series

on Brethren in Christ doctrine.

On the Saturday before his death, John went to a baseball game in Chicago with part of his family. On Sunday he attended services at Nappanee and with his wife celebrated their twenty-ninth wedding anniversary. During the following week he was present at meetings of the Commission on Christian Education Literature, did some gardening, watched his sons play in a church softball game, helped Alice Grace entertain a guest, and visited the factory where one of his sons had summer employment. His week was almost a composite of his life.

On the morning of August 24, 1979, he drove to the Nappanee church to participate in a promotion meeting for the Foundation Series curriculum. Shortly after entering the building he suffered a heart attack and died immediately.

One of John's favorite Bible passages contains God's call to Abraham to sacrifice Isaac. In referring to these verses, John would speak of the point of no return—the object of faith is commitment, not mere belief. John's favorite definition of faith, repeated many times, was: "Faith is not belief in spite of evidence, but in life lived in scorn of consequences." Those words may serve as a fitting commentary on his own life and ministry.

Part 2
Editorials
for the
Brethren in Christ

The Christian Citizen

A national election is an occasion of soul searching for thoughtful citizens. This is the time for reflection on the life of the nation and an opportunity to conform or alter that nation's direction.

For a Christian this occasion has a deeper dimension. For him judgments should not be made on the basis of party loyalty or self interest. His ultimate decisions as a citizen are based upon his overarching allegiance to Christ.

The relation of a Christian to the state has never been clearly spelled out in the Brethren in Christ Church. We recognize the role of government in God's order, yet we are aware of the two realms of God's activity—the state and the church. Our Anabaptist heritage and the knowledge that our forefathers suffered for their faith at the hands of the state keeps us from identifying too closely the role of the church and the state. This keeps us, as well, a little uncertain as to the role of the Christian as a citizen of his country.

As Brethren in Christ in the United States and Canada, we do well to recall the price our fathers paid at the hands of the state. We should also recall that it was the refusal by the Christians to bow at the Emperor's statue that resulted in the bloody persecution of the early centuries. We need to remind ourselves at this time in a special way what our fathers and the early Christians knew—that Christ alone is Lord.

So when we face a national event, such as an election, this supreme loyalty must determine one's response. For some this may well mean the traditional attitude of the Brethren in Christ—as little involvement as necessary. Thus taxes are paid, respect is given, prayers are offered, laws are obeyed. But to serve in the government or to vote for its officials goes beyond that which a citizen of the New Kingdom should go.

Many Brethren in Christ, however, have moved one step away from the traditional position and exercise the right to vote. For this group Christ must continue to be Lord. This lordship needs to find expression in a concrete and practical way.

As Christians we should understand the depth of selfishness that governs so much of our action. We are for lower taxes at the expense of education when we have property but no children. As laborers we favor minimum wage laws; as an employer we want open shop legislation. Our supreme allegiance as Christians, however, should place the national welfare above that of class or special interest.

One of the tasks of government is to protect society from the evil doer—the maintenance of order under law. Government has a concomitant responsibility to protect the individual from society. So we have our police force to protect society, and the courts to protect the individual. These must be kept in balance. As Christians we would do well to recall the concern of the prophets and of Christ for the individual and listen for the note of justice in the theme of law and order.

As Brethren in Christ we ought to be suspect of those whose answer to world problems is found so easily in military force. We should know that they which take the sword will perish by the sword. Our sons and our daughters have planted the cross in Africa, and Asia, and Latin America and have shown love in Christ's name around the world. We should take a second thought before we support a platform that is enamored of military force and overly impressed with the role of the United States in the affairs of the world.

Our franchise should be exercised with the conviction that a man's leadership is tied closely to his character. We have every right to expect those whom we elect to be men of honesty and integrity; whose motives are unselfish and whose sense of responsibility goes beyond the electorate to a Supreme Being to whom they are ultimately accountable.

Whether we exercise our franchise or not, we are aware of the critical nature of our time. May we as citizens of whatever nation it may be seek God's face for a revival of righteousness which exalteth a nation.

The Light and the Bushel

The Brethren in Christ are known as one of the historic peace churches. Article XVIII of the Constitution and By Laws affirms this historic postion, ". . . participation in military service is inconsistent with the teaching of Scripture concerning nonresistance." This historic and official position has been supported by actions of the General Conference and the counselling of young men to choose alternate service in lieu of the military.

It is my observation that we are more certain of the role of our

young men in the practice of this doctrine than we are in its
proclamation. We are not clear where nonresistance, especially as
it relates to the refusal to bear arms, fits into the call to repentance.
We are hesitant to proclaim it for fear of alienating those who are
not yet prepared to receive it.

Our proclamation of this position is tempered not only by our
evangelistic concern but also by our pastoral commitment. We
find a tension between the prophetic and the pastoral roles. In our
congregations and in our communities there are individuals who
need our spiritual ministries but who are deeply committed to a
position other than nonresistance. This commitment is either
philosophical or exists because a member of the family is identified with the military. It is a wise and courageous pastor who can
preach, clearly and definitely, on the full implications of nonresistance when in the audience there are families with members in
the service or families who have lost sons in Vietnam. Nor is this
made any easier when the nonresistant position appears to have
acquired some strange bed-fellows and when, on the other hand,
the conservative wing of the Christian church supports the
military.

In contrast to what I sense as some uncertainty and hesitancy on
our part as a denomination is the growing uneasiness of the
Christian church in general with the traditional position which
permitted and even encouraged Christians to support their country through military service.

Indeed the events of the past few years, brought so graphically
and uncensored into our lives through various media, have caused
all thoughtful and sensitive people to see the futility and brutality
of war. Both within and without the Christian church there is a
new openness to the message of nonresistance as a way to confront
evil and hatred.

I question if there ever was a time more receptive to this teaching. It may be high time for those of us who hold this doctrine to
see it not as a *demand* of the gospel but as part of the *Good News
itself.* It is time to remove the bushel, trim the wick, and let the
light of the doctrine of nonresistant love shine in a war-weary and
violence-filled world.

But we need to do some homework. There are some questions we
need to ask in all candor and answers we need to seek, such as the
following:

Where in the proclamation of the Gospel and the call to repentance does the doctrine of nonresistance come in?

Is our understanding of nonresistance as expressed in the refusal
of military service an optional act of obedience?

How and when in our concern for personal salvation do we confront the seeker with the implications of this doctrine?

How do we resolve the tension between the prophetic voice and a pastoral concern?

What is our understanding of the responsibility of a Christian as a citizen to the state which is ordained of God to maintain order and restrain evil?

Let no one interpret this concern as a call to legalism. Rather it is a call to reassess our stewardship of the message with which the Brethren in Christ, along with a number of other fellowships, have been entrusted. For who knows but for such an hour as this we have been called.

Unscheduling a Revival

As I read the numerous reports of the Asbury College revival I glanced over the institutions to see if our college had been one moved by this revival. But the name of Messiah College did not appear. Now before someone is tempted to be critical of the college I should add that hundreds of churches were also affected in the weeks following February 3 but I learned of no Brethren in Christ congregations significantly affected. If there has been one, the bulletins are strangely silent.

As I ponder these facts I ask, how can it be that the Brethren in Christ with our evangelical identification, our heritage of revivalism, and our emphasis upon experience have been seemingly untouched by these events? I am not certain that I know. I would venture several observations.

We are basically a cautious and conservative people. There have been in our history experiences of dramatic and emotional movements that have taught us to be cautious. A seminary president close to the Asbury revival was asked to give an evaluation of the moving and is quoted as saying, "Give me thirty days and I will be able to tell you if it is authentic." We would probably as a group need at least as much time.

Another reason that we as a denomination—colleges, congregations and individuals—are not in the vanguard of such a moving may be due to our understanding of the Christian life. We have a conviction, born of our understanding of Scripture, that the Christian life is more than experience. Experience is essential but is validated in a life of obedience, discipleship, sacrifice and love. We are justifiably cautious of a moving that emphasizes experience as both the beginning and the end, the foundation and the super-structure of the Christian life. In this respect our problem would not be with the fact of the revival but of its lack of depth.

Our caution, beginning as a virtue, can become a sin. We are commanded to try the spirits. We are warned of false prophets who have all the trappings of authenticity but fail the crucial test. But we can spend our lifetime sitting in judgment of movements and never be identified with them. We can always wait for God to authenticate a new thing and never commit ourselves to it.

I recall a friend of mine who would never accept currency larger than a five-dollar bill. He reasoned that in this way his chance of receiving counterfeit money was almost nil. He assumed that no one would bother to counterfeit one- and five-dollar bills. So out of fear of the counterfeit he dealt all his life in small currency.

There are many Christians whose fear of the counterfeit intimi-dates them from receiving the genuine. Their fear of wild fire prevents their receiving the true fire that sets them ablaze. It is a serious sin to receive light and not to walk in it. But the ultimate tragedy is to become so critical and judgmental that light is sus-pected of being darkness and truth is interpreted as error.

Our understanding of the Christian life which goes beyond experience is a valid insight. But we ignore the primacy of expe-rience and the reality of the emotional aspect of our life at our peril. We cannot built a life of service and Christian love on a foundation which lacks an adequate relationship with God. The question of forgiveness and reconciliation and the new life born of the Spirit cannot be ignored. As important as it is to see the Christian life as more than experience, it is absolutely essential to have the reality of a personal encounter with God.

The Meaning of Brotherhood

In the early hours of Thursday morning, April 15, 1971 the Auditorium-Gymnasium on the Niagara Christian College cam-pus burned. Two other fires at about the same time and in proximity to the campus strongly suggest that the fires were the result of arson.

The structure, built in 1951, not only served the College but was also used by the Niagara Holiness Campmeeting as the site of its annual summer camp. It was the place of meeting for the General Conference when the Canadian Conference was the host. In addition, many other groups requiring the commodious facilities of the building used it throughout the year.

At a special regional conference held on Saturday, May 1, the Canadian Conference decided without dissent to rebuild. To provide the facilities which are planned will approach the $150,000 ceiling which the conference placed on the rebuilding program. Insurance carried on the building amounted to $35,000. The ceiling figure placed on the rebuilding program will cover the building of a new structure, replacing the lost equipment, and adding some additional facilities such as classrooms, which are needed in the college program.

All of these statements and facts fail to convey the sense of loss and shock to the Canadian constituency. An essential facility for the college and the church was lost. The financial load upon a conference of 1,500 members is a heavy one. Memories spiritual and sentimental are part of the charred ruins.

This is where the name "Brethren in Christ" takes on meaning. When I learned of the loss shortly after its occurrence, and then again on Saturday as I stood with Bishop Climenhaga and looked at the charred ruins and the empty basement which alone remain, I knew that if brotherhood had any meaning, now was the time.

Many scriptures come to mind which speak to this event: "And whether one member suffers, all the members suffer with it;" "Bear ye one another's burdens and so fulfill the law of Christ;" "For I mean not that other men be eased, and ye burdened; But by an equality, that now at this time your abundance may be a supply for their want, that their abundance may be a supply for your want; that there may be equality." Put into modern terms this simply means that what to the Canadian church would be a heavy burden becomes a bearable load when shared by the brotherhood.

I understand that by the time this issue of the *Visitor* arrives in our readers' homes the Board of Administration will have taken action relative to the response of the church at large in sharing this load. Our confidence in the brethren who serve on this Board leads us to believe that an organized opportunity will be given so all can share.

And as we share there are two considerations which will add a spiritual dimension to this experience: first, this should be a brotherhood effort—a grass roots response with everyone sharing and not only those who can "afford" it; and second, our giving should bear the mark of sacrifice. This should come out of the nine-tenths rather than the tithe.. Hopefully no church board or agency will need to bear this added giving.

Pentecost resulted in numerous expressions by those who were touched by that experience. There was a boldness, a new dynamic, and a contagious joy in their lives. There is one expression of the early church, however, that does not usually receive the same attention in our reference to Pentecost—in fact we are almost apologetic for it: but it is recorded that "All that believed . . . had all things common. And sold their possessions and goods, and parted them to all men, *as every man had need."*

In our tradition we have attempted to combine the concept of Pentecost and of brotherhood. We now have the opportunity to prove the reality of each and the potential of both.

I Have Faith in Messiah College

A college is many things. It is foremost—or at least should be—an institution of learning. A Christian college should be more, but it ought not to be less. Institutions of the church—missions, camps, homes—each has its distinct purpose. The college is no different. In its ministry to the church and the world it has a unique purpose. This purpose is learning.

My faith in Messiah College is strong because the college has kept this purpose in mind. Its academic integrity is recognized by those responsible for accrediting institutions of learning. Messiah is highly respected by peer institutions. I need not apologize to my sons nor need they apologize to their friends for a second-rate academic experience at Messiah. Piety should be highly regarded in a Christian college, but it is not a substitute for learning.

Ivy grows up the sides of Old Main and a covered bridge spans the Minnemingo. The college is aware of its heritage and proud of its traditions but is not bound by them. Messiah is alive. The college is creative. This is seen in the establishing of a campus in Philadelphia across Broad Street from Temple University. At Messiah, students can have the best of two worlds—the smaller Christian caring community and the benefits of a large university.

The "aliveness" is seen in the review of curriculum and the providing of commodious facilities such as the Campus Center and the proposed Learning Resources Center. Course offerings and majors are related to the Brethren in Christ understanding of the Christian life and service. All of this may keep the observer in somewhat of a daze but it guards against academic stagnation.

My faith in Messiah is strengthened because of the institution's financial soundness. Messiah's budgets have been consistently balanced in a day when many colleges are living off of their capital and others have closed their doors. The student body has been growing when many college enrollments are declining. On the basis of the college's financial position it is worthy of our continued support.

We would do well to thank God for competent administrators and a concerned Board of Trustees who have guided the college wisely during these critical, financial years.

My faith is undergirded by the quality and the commitment of the faculty. We have a faculty that is academically competent and spiritually committed. They are at Messiah because of what Messiah is. Members of the faculty serve on denominational boards and commissions. They minister in our churches. The college has the stature it has because those who served on its faculty took their professional obligations seriously and their Christian commitment with equal dedication. I find it no small satisfaction to have my sons study under such a faculty.

I have faith in Messiah because here is the atmosphere for spiritual growth. Piety is encouraged but not forced. Disciplines for spiritual growth are structured. Bible study and prayer groups are available. Piety is not something divorced from learning and the classroom. There is no dichotomy between head and heart.

We are a believers' church. This means that those who are members should be so because of their own decision and choice. This choice is to be made knowledgeably and responsibly. Now, most of our children come into the church at an age when the options and alternatives are really not options and alternatives. On the basis of an experience of forgiveness they are encouraged to identify with the local fellowship. There is always the possibility that this identification with the church is never a genuine decision based upon choices but rather one based on our family ties. No "Choose you this day whom ye will serve" is really faced.

The college fills a need in resolving this tension between a childhood conversion and a believers' church. Here in a loving and committed community, at a level of greater maturity, the student can choose between the options open. No one knows the meaning of courage who has not experienced fear. No one knows the meaning of faith who has not known doubt. No one can make a real decision unless real options are open. In college, options are open. In college, options become real. At Messiah, the decision is made within a community of Christian love and faith.

It may seem that I have been carried away by my long relationship to the college and that I see Messiah as one place where the millennial age has come. That is hardly the case. Messiah is not the perfect institution. There are none. Our homes are not perfect. Our congregations are not perfect. Nor is that other college or Bible School you heard about perfect.

Messiah is part of the church, fulfilling its ministry to and for the church. I am thankful for the college. I believe Messiah is worthy of our support and prayers, and of our sons and daughters.

We Are a General Conference

To meet as a general conference means more than meeting as a church-wide convention. We meet in General Conference because we are a general conference. This means that as congregations we are bound to one another in a relationship that is mutually binding and mutually supportive.

Our General Conference grew out of our origin. As members of the initial congregations moved from their Lancaster County birthplace to neighboring counties, into Canada, across the Alleghenies to Ohio and Indiana, and then westward to California, they established congregations which they saw as extensions of the brotherhood. The older, established congregations and districts sent brethren to visit these newer and scattered ones. These scattered and distant congregations were considered to be part of the body—they too were River Brethren, later to be known as Brethren in Christ.

They counseled together in matters of doctrine and life They searched together for the meaning of obedience. They believed that God was consistent and truth would not be one thing to one congregation and something else to another. They believed that the church had a responsibility to interpret God's Word, and they felt more secure in the church interpreting Scripture than for each one to interpret the Scriptures on his own.

Missions, benevolence, schools, a church paper became concerns of the entire brotherhood. The church moved too fast for some, too slow for others. There were some losses. But the denomination has continued. Although not large, it is alive and well. It has been held together by those ministries we do together, by a common understanding of Christian living and Christian experience, and by a commitment to biblical truths held dear and held in common.

As congregations become deeply involved in the local ministry and are able to provide a self-contained program, they may develop a sense of self-sufficiency. But congregations need to be identified with a larger meaningful entity—a fellowship with which they feel a common bond in the understanding of the Christian life, doctrine, and practice.

There are few really "independent" congregations. Even those which claim to be "independent" or "congregational" or "community" find types of associations which support them and through which they widen their ministry.

The possibility of regionalism is as real with us as is congregationalism. As a denomination we are widely scattered geographically. The sense of isolation on the one hand and the concentration of membership and institutions on the other could lead to our thinking and our planning becoming regional rather than general (denominational).

The regional conferences are administrative structures within the denomination. They, as well, provide a level of fellowship midway between the congregations and the denomination. The welfare of each region—its pastoral needs, institutional benefits, programs for fellowship and nurture—must be the concern of the General Conference and the general boards. When a regional conference is weak, the entire church is weakened. When a regional conference is strengthened, the church is stronger.

With our thoughts directed at this time to the General Conference we must remember that the congregation is the growing edge of the church. It is there where the action is. The regional conferences exist to facilitate the ministry of the congregation and to communicate and channel the supportive ministries of the denomination. The General Conference exists to serve the congregations—to discover through congregational representation the mind of the church and hopefully the will of God in areas of doctrine, and life and ministry. Although it is the nature of the General Conference that these decisions have a binding effect upon the congregations, the decisions are in fact made by congregational representatives.

May we come with faith in each other and trust in God, open to the counsel of our brethren and sisters, sensitive to the Spirit of God, and seeking for the mind of Christ.

Observations on Missions

Within the past few years the "mission churches" in India, Zambia, and Rhodesia have become autonomous Brethren in Christ general conferences. How does the church in North America relate to these new churches and what does that mean for the mission of the church and the need for missionaries?

We all—members, pastors, administrators—need to keep change and biblical commands in proper perspective. In interest of this effort we suggest the following:

First: The changes which are related to the emergence of national autonomous churches are changes for which we should rejoice. This is indeed what missions is all about—a ministry and a program which results in churches that become mature, autonomous, and mission-minded.

So when we learn of the church in India or Zambia or Rhodesia assuming responsibility for its own life and destiny, with the resultant change in the role and the numbers of North American missionaries, this is a time for thanksgiving and not alarm. This is advance and not retreat. It may be difficult to express what is happening to missionaries, to programs, and to budgets without suggesting retrenchment, but we dare not interpret this as the dying of the missionary effort. Pastors, itinerant missionaries, mission and church administrations, letter-writers, and editors must exercise care not to report retreat when what is happening is advance.

Second: The Great Commission has not been rescinded. The changes resulting from our recognition of autonomous General Conferences in what were formerly regarded as "mission fields" do not nullify the Great Commission nor circumscribe its geographical or cultural boundaries. The world is Christ's parish and into it we are commanded to go.

If perchance we have placed the accent on the "go" in years past, let us not in our reaction err in becoming only local in our vision and immobile in our mission. The church that follows Christ in missionary obedience will go where he leads. All the world is his and he will lead us across national and cultural boundaries.

Third: The New Testament pattern reflects a special and close relationship between the parent church and the new church. A wise parent will expect and anticipate the day when the child becomes mature and will take responsibility for his own destiny. At that point the parent respects this autonomy but will continue to carry a concern—a concern that is special and which expresses itself in availability. So it should be with the church.

The comparison between parent and child and the older and the newer church is obvious and valid. Perhaps a new term must be found to express this relationship. The term missionary does not seem to quite fit this new reality. We are equals, not just before God as has always been the case, but in ecclesiastical relationship as well.

Fourth: We need to find new fields of missionary service. One can assume that the demand for personnel and funds will change as autonomy is granted. The reservoir of missionary dedication within the Brethren in Christ Church needs to have new avenues and opportunities of expression. The maturing of a church in one location is not the completion of the missionary task but is in fact one chapter in its ongoing. Resources which are released as a mission field becomes a church can be used at another location to continue to make disciples and to establish other churches.

I have a vision of the chief administrators of the several Brethren in Christ General Conferences visiting each other's churches—not as parent to child or as administrator to those administered—but as representatives of autonomous General Conferences—as equals in the growing number of Brethren in Christ General Conferences around the world.

This is what it is all about.

A More Excellent Way

One of the numerous advantages of denominational identification is that it provides answers to the questions which come to one's mind when appeals are received. In the case of the Brethren in Christ, there is a wide range of ministries, camping, orphanages, retirement and nursing homes, evangelism, radio, schools, food, medicine, pastoral training, and extension churches.

We know the people who serve and administer in our institutions and congregations. I recently saw the Missions Photo Album, which includes national leaders of the churches in Japan, India, Zambia, Rhodesia and Nicaragua, as well as the North Americans who are serving with them and in ministries at home. These are people we know—many on a first-name basis. I recently spent a week on Messiah's Campus and several days at Niagara Christian College. I know the people at Labish Village, Messiah Home, Navajo Mission and Messiah Children's Home. I know the administrators at the Missions office and the colleges.

These are our—your and my—brethren and sisters. They share with the rest of the denomination a common understanding of ministry and the Christian life. We inherit a tradition of sacrifice, frugality and industry. We take both the Great Commandments and the Great Commission seriously.

We do not mean to suggest that all missions and causes except Brethren in Christ causes are suspect. There are certainly many good and worthy causes outside the denomination and we will have some we will wish to support. There are also many Christians outside the denomination who do not have denominational causes to which they carry an obligation. These outside causes become channels for their giving and support.

It is required of us that we be certain that we invest the Lord's money with faithfulness. Faithfulness calls us to be as judicious in the investment of the Lord's money as we would be with our own.

Since it is Someone else's money, we should exercise even more care.

Pastors are People

The Brethren in Christ do not have a long pastoral tradition in the usual understanding of the pastoral ministry.

I entered the pastorate a little more than twenty years ago. I supported my family by full-time secular employment (44 hours a week). I served the church during the evenings, Saturday afternoons, and Sundays. This personal item is in itself not really the point. What is significant is that at that time—two decades ago— the great majority of our churches were served by either a multiple-ministry or by a minister designated as a pastor but who either fully or partially supported his family by other employment.

Now this pattern was followed not primarily because of the size of a congregation but because of the nature of the congregation and the ministry. More often than not the minister (or ministers) was chosen from within the membership by a vote of the congregation. He would be expected to serve in addition to continuing in his vocation. There were exceptions to this pattern, but they were the exception rather than the rule.

There has been a substantial change in these twenty years. Now even the smaller congregation wants a pastor who can give at least part-time to the pastoral duties. The goal of the larger congregation is a pastor who can give full-time.

No longer do congregations look within their own membership for their minister. They call one from outside the congregation. What is more significant, perhaps, is that the men whom they call are men who have received "a call" to the ministry—not from the church as in former years, but from an inner personal awareness. In addition, many of these men in response to their call have taken training in preparation for the ministry.

This has been a significant change in a relatively few years. I am not certain that this recent change against a tradition a century and a half old has been made without some cost. Have we given careful thought to our understanding of the pastoral ministry and the congregation's attitude towards the supported, God-called, trained minister?

Let me make some random observations and raise some questions which bear upon this relationship and attitude.

There should be a mutual understanding of ministry and expectations. Each pastor comes with his strengths and his weaknesses. Hopefully he is aware of these and sees his ministry accordingly. He surely needs to correct his weaknesses, but he as well needs to use his strengths.

If there is this understanding, both pastor and congregation can get on with the ministry, majoring in strength, supportive in weakness, grateful for each other, together making up the body of Christ. There are few "complete pastors." If both pastor and people recognize this, a major potential of disappointment has been taken care of.

The congregation's expectations of the pastor need to be realistic. He is neither omnipresent nor omniscient. He does not know of every need and situation in the congregation. Nor can he be at more than one place at a time. Most pastors are not psychic. Their knowledge comes only through the normal channels and media of communication. They find out that someone is ill in the same manner as the doctor does.

The pastor is not the servant of the congregation. (If I were writing primarily to pastors I might accent that statement a bit differently.) Unfortunately the relative newness of pastoral support makes it easy to take this position. When the minister (pastor) earned his living at a full-time vocation it was assumed that he could not do all the tasks that were there to be done. The members felt a responsibility. But now we pay our pastor. We reason that he should be able to do these tasks plus others of which we were earlier not even aware.

One cannot emphasize enough the scriptural vision of the pastor as one whose gift is to equip the members for ministry. A mark of a good pastor is the involvement of the members. Both pastor and congregation should be alert to the danger of the pastor becoming involved in the administrative routine, and indeed the outreach routine, to the point where he neglects those ministries which he is uniquely prepared and called to do.

The family and home life of the pastor must be respected. The parsonage is the home of the pastor's family and not the parish house of the church. The parsonage should be—both in its structure and maintenance—a credit to the church. In congregational decisions which affect the parsonage, the woman's touch and taste should be reflected.

The congregation should understand that the first responsibility of the pastor's wife is to him and to their children. The nature of the pastor's ministry places extra demands upon the wife and the family. She should not be expected to be the church secretary or even the husband's secretary in addition to these home duties.

It can be expected that the pastor's family will share in the life and ministry of the church as the other families do. But to expect more from the pastor's family than we do of our own is to misunderstand the ministry of all believers and to deny the integrity of the parsonage family life.

Congregation and pastor are both members of the body of Christ, different in function and diverse in ministry but one in purpose. The purpose is to be responsive to the Head, even Christ, and to be his presence and body in this world.

The Holy Life

I recently shared in a brief seminar on John Wesley and on the sixteenth century Anabaptists. It is generally recognized that the doctrinal roots of the Brethren in Christ reach into both of these theological traditions.

It is assumed that to John Wesley we owe our understanding of sanctification and to the early Anabaptists our emphasis upon brotherhood and discipleship. What is not as commonly recognized is that both Wesley and the Anabaptists were vitally concerned with holiness. With John Wesley holiness was an experience of perfect love and purity of heart. With the Anabaptists the emphasis was upon holiness of life and obedient living.

It would be unfair to Wesley to suggest that he was unconcerned about holy living. His own early days of spiritual pilgrimage and the classes he established for his converts are clear evidence that holiness of life was not ignored. But he is remembered for his teaching of an experience of the heart which enabled a man to wholly love God.

Likewise to assume that the early Anabaptists were really sixteenth century Pharisees living a legalistic lifestyle is to misunderstand what had occurred. Central to Anabaptism was regeneration. God's grace went beyond justification. It went beyond imputed righteousness to an imparted righteousness that radically changed a man.

Let me observe that for the Anabaptists the threat to Christian faith and obedience was the world. They were aware of the two kingdoms—the kingdom of God and the kingdom of the world. They were called out of one into the other. This meant that they were called to deny the values which the world lived by—power, self-seeking, the love of money, pride, and lordship. These were in direct opposition to the pattern of the kingdom of God where love and servanthood and the cross were the values to live by. These early Anabaptists were not very optimistic about the world.

Now John Wesley had a more optimistic view of society. But he was more pessimistic about man. For John Wesley, it was the flesh—that root of bitterness, the enmity against God—which needed to be dealt with if a man was to attain unto holiness. This need could and should be dealt with in an experience subsequent to conversion. It was this crisis—the second crisis—that became the great concern of Wesley. Heart purity and perfect love were his passion.

It is not our purpose to ask if the Anabaptists were correct in their attitude toward the world and naive in their understanding of man. Nor is it our purpose to ask if John Wesley was truly biblical in his view of man and too naive in his view of society. We will let that to the scholars.

We do want to point òut that the Bible sees both the flesh and the world as enemies of holy living. The one sabotages our efforts from within. The other allures us from without.

The Bible speaks clearly of man's rebel spirit. The Bible is clear that God wishes and is able to do more about sin than forgive it. A theology that ignores sin by dealing with sins is neither true to the Scriptures nor adequate for life.

The Bible is just as clear about the danger from without—the lure of the world. The desire for position and power, the love of money and pleasure, the use of force, and the denial of the cross are marks of the world. "If any man loves the world, the love of the Father is not in him," states the Apostle John.

We should be grateful for these two emphases in our heritage. We need to constantly nourish and safeguard both. It is easy to become occupied with one to the extent that we ignore the other. Intrigued with the enemy within we awake to find ourselves captured by the one without. Very much aware of the subtleties and attractiveness of the world we succumb to the enemy within.

Two Bicentennials
1976 and 1978

It is an interesting coincidence that the United States Bicentennial (1976) and the observance of the Two Hundredth Anniversary of the founding of the Brethren in Christ (1978) should come so close together. I had not been aware that at about the same time the Thirteen Colonies were declaring their independence, a small group of Christians in Lancaster County, Pennsylvania, were declaring their dependence.

The proximity in time of these two events gives us opportunity and indeed the obligation to examine the meaning of each and our observance of the occasions.

How does a church that rejects violence and war observe the bicentennial of a nation born out of an armed revolution and held together by a bloody and tragic civil war? Equally crucial is the question: How does a church whose members live under different flags regard its national ties at a time when one of these nations observes a national anniversary?

It should be obvious that as a denomination we should play the Bicentennial (1976) theme in a very low key. I could hope that the General Conference gives none or only passing recognition to this national anniversary. (I am glad we did not decide to go to Philadelphia for our 1976 General conference.) This is the opportunity to emphasize the multinational character of the Brethren in Christ. If we are to observe a bicentennial let us emphasize the covenant of dependence and interdependence, brotherhood and mutual support, servanthood and evangelism, calling men to a kingdom that knows no national boundaries—the bicentennial of 1978.

United States congregations may not desire to pass over the 1976 bicentennial quite so lightly. Members will be confronted daily with the varied aspects of the celebration. The church needs to speak to men in the context of their daily experiences. Certainly this will be one of those experiences. This occasion will be an opportunity and a peril—an opportunity to proclaim a prophetic word and the temptation to allow patriotism to blur our values and priorities.

We should be wary of allowing patriotism and the passage of time to glorify a violent revolution that gave birth to the United States. Whatever the benefits which independence brought in opportunities and freedoms we will do well not to glorify in our past that which we decry in the present and which we reject on biblical and Christian grounds—violent revolution.

A centennial or a bicentennial is not traditionally the time to take a critical look at the past. These are celebrations to highlight the positive. However, if we are to recall the past with profit it will be necessary to view our history with objectivity and candor. Our present problems will be better understood from the perspective of history. In many cases the roots of these problems go back to events and even injustices in our past. An honest confession is not only good for the soul, it is oft times good for the situation and the solution. The racial issue—blacks and Indians—is a case in point.

We need to be on our guard lest in observing the bicentennial we betray our faith. I may be mistaken but I predict that some aspects of our history which will be praised will not stand before the bar of biblical justice and righteousness. Even if we do not expect the unregenerate state to live by the Sermon on the Mount we should beware of glorifying from Christian pulpits sub-Christian values, actions and solutions.

There are many noble concepts of freedom and justice which

have come down through these two hundred years—concepts which found expression in the documents associated with the founding of the nation. The separation of church and state is one of these. What is separated by law should be separate in fact. The possibility of the state using the church in support of its policies is an ever present danger. The God of Scripture is the God of the whole earth. He is not a national or tribal deity. I confess to some misgivings when a Christian convocation begins its service with a pledge of allegiance to the national flag. I have similar feelings when I see a national flag displayed in a Christian church.

As Brethren in Christ the bicentennial of 1978 should have much deeper significance than that of 1976. These two events in proximity to each other will give us the occasion to reflect upon these two kingdoms in which we hold our citizenship. This should provide an opportunity to examine our responsibilities to each and the conflicts and tension which arise from this dual citizenship. This will be the opportunity to determine which has the ultimate claim and how that claim is expressed.

I Thank God for MCC

When I read the Gospels and realize that Jesus' call to follow leads the church and his disciples to a ministry to the hungry, the homeless and the sick, I thank God that he has raised up an organization that helps me and my church carry out this part of the teachings of Christ.

When I read in the papers and see on television the devastation left by an earthquake or hurricane or war, and my compassion urges me to do something to minister, I am thankful that this emotion can find expression in action through the Mennonite Central Committee. The peril of becoming insensitive and calloused through inaction is lessened because I do have a means of response. I thank God for MCC!

When I am tempted to spiritualize my Christian faith and separate the ministry to people in terms of soul and body, when like the Levite and the priest in Jesus' memorable parable I become too busy with religious duties to minister to the bruised and heathen,

then I thank God for MCC and for reminding me of the biblical teaching of the indivisibility of man and the wholeness of the gospel.

When I live in comfort in my air-conditioned office and spend time deciding which suit I should wear today, when my trouble is too much food rather than too little, I thank God for MCC and for keeping before me the picture of Lazarus and Dives and for the subtle suggestion of whom I most closely resemble. Like pain, MCC is blessing in disguise, for when it hurts it is usually the truth. Even for this I thank God!

When some things need to be said that run counter to society's values and even counter to the position held by some Christians, when our dependence upon military strength is contrasted with our claim of faith in God and people become the pawns in the struggle for power, I thank God for MCC. It is so easy for the church to evade the sensitive aspects of the gospel and emphasize those which are widely held and without controversy. We need the prophetic voice within the church which MCC provides. Even when I do not agree, I thank God for MCC.

When heart-touching appeals for support come to my desk or plead with me from the pages of a magazine, I thank God for MCC. I have confidence that the financial aid I wish to share will, in the hands of MCC, be used with wisdom and Christian perspective— in the name of Christ.

In a day when national barriers seem to be rising higher and higher and the missionary is regarded at times with some suspicion, I thank God that we are identified with an organization that has had some success in breaking these national barriers and reflecting the fact that the Christian church is above culture and national identity and that as Christians our love is extended even to the enemy.

When the usual response to a need is the writing of a check or the passing of a resolution, I thank God for MCC and its emphasis upon personal involvement with people in need. The sun never sets on the ministry and ministers of MCC. Worldwide needs have been responded to by a worldwide ministry of love and caring and Christian motivation. Not only can I be present with my gifts but also in the hearts and hands of Christians who minister in both my name and the name of Christ.

I thank God for MCC. May God bless its ministry, sustain its ministers, and safeguard its Christian motivation.

The Message and Church Growth

A respected churchman, in a recent conversation, observed that unless the Brethren in Christ change some of their emphases we may as well forget about church growth. I suspect that one of the reasons for this very pointed observation was to obtain my reaction. I believe, however, that this brother wrestles with the tension between our understanding of faithfulness to the Scriptures and our responsibility to the Great Commission.

I question if he is alone in sensing this tension. If I thought that he alone had this concern I would not use an editorial to respond to him. I suspect that any concerned pastor or layman seeing and hearing about church growth in other communions searches his soul as to why this may not be happening in his own congregation.

The person referred to in the beginning of this editorial assumes that church growth is a proper concern for the Brethren in Christ. He is right. It is a proper concern. Church growth is more than evangelism. The wide difference between conversions and church accessions which was our pattern for too many years hopefully is past. The Great Commission is not fulfilled by evangelism alone. We need to bring converts into the fellowship of the church.

Growth may not be the only expression of life but it surely is a legitimate one. Numerical increase is a legitimate expression of growth. The compassion which our Lord expressed and the concern which the apostles reflected will find expression in reaching people.

As long as there are those in our communities outside of Christ, no church or pastor should be satisfied for the congregation's membership to remain the same year after year. If numerical growth is not taking place, it is time to ask some serious questions about the impact (the witness) which the congregation is making in the community.

The other assumption which is reflected in my friend's statement is that the message a church proclaims affects that church's ability to grow. Even more precise is the assumption that the message of the Brethren in Christ has restricted and may continue to restrict its growth.

It is easy to assume that the reason for non-growth is the message preached and the demands which that message makes. It is less threatening to look at the message and at membership demands than to look at the image which the church has in the community or the spiritual vitality or lack of spiritual life within the congregation.

We do need to examine our message and the interpretation of that message. If there are elements which cannot be supported by a Christ-centered understanding of the Scriptures, this would call for some evaluation. Within the Brethren in Christ, however, it should be assumed that no major deviations from traditional understanding of the Scripture be made unilaterally. Such evaluation is done by the brotherhood.

It could be that the brotherhood in study and consultation will find new light and may temper traditional teaching by a new understanding of God's Word and will. Cultural and ethnic shadings of the message should not be discarded lightly but may need to submit to the mission of the church and the overall theme of the gospel.

The easy assumption that growth is the measure of the message needs to be examined. There are other influences which bear upon the growth of a group. To soften biblical demands in the interest of growth is both unfaithful and dishonest. The church can gain the whole world and lose its own soul.

If we read the Gospels and recall the ministry of our Lord, we will be better prepared for the realities of church growth. The crowds pressed upon Christ for the benefits of healing and food and to witness the miracles. When some saw in him indications that he might be the political deliverer for whom they looked, they were attracted to him. But when he spoke of denial, cross bearing, and the cross itself, it was only a minority that remained. In fact, he spoke about the narrow gate and the strait way which leads to life and the few who find it.

This is no pleading for small, ingrown, self-righteous, unconcerned congregations, nor for pious ethnic ghettos. We are not called to maintain ethnic purity in our congregations or denomination. This is not an excuse for writing off our world and our communities before God does. This is not a call to freeze our interpretation of the gospel in 18th or 19th or mid-20th century forms and to equate cultural traditions with scriptural revelation.

It is a call to be faithful messengers of God's grace and his call. We must beware of offering cheap grace—justification of sin rather than of the sinner and forgiveness without repentance. We dare not assume that by softening the biblical message we can be more redemptive in our ministry.

If we think that certain aspects of the Brethren in Christ message make growth difficult, this could say more about us than about the message. Seventh-day Adventists could well believe that their emphasis upon Saturday as the day of rest and worship is a substantial hindrance of growth. Can you imagine one of their pastors suggesting that they change their day to Sunday in order to reach more people? Convinced that the seventh day as the Sabbath is a very significant part of their message, they are able to present the message convincingly, and church growth results.

Finally, it is important that we see the demands of the gospel and the hard sayings of Jesus as essential elements of the gospel. Our need to forgive others is just as much a part of the gospel as God's forgiveness of us. We are so influenced by the world's values that we find anything which runs counter to these values as bad news. Surely fidelity in marriage is better news than profligacy; sobriety is better news than drunkenness; forgiveness of others is better news than resentment; servanthood is better than lordship; death to self is better than retaliation; obedience to God is better than enslavement to self or Satan.

It would be interesting to speculate what would have been our approach to the rich young ruler and our reaction to his response. Jesus felt deeply about the young man's refusal to follow but there is no indication that he even considered altering the message to gain a soul. In reality one does not gain souls by watering down the message. One may, perchance, gain numbers.

Roots

Newspaper columnists, magazine editors, sociologists and psychologists will no doubt have a field-day analyzing the reason and meaning of the phenomenal appeal which Alex Haley's book *Roots* and ABC's television presentation of it has had.

Apparently there is a basic—perhaps subconscious—longing in man to know who he is. This knowledge is somehow linked to his roots. Who we are and to whom we belong demand more than the present moment.

One of the problems of our society is a loss of community. The "melting pot" theory which encouraged immigrants to our shores to cut their roots and become part of the mass has had its price—a loss of meaningful community and identity.

Roots are without question a Christian concern. Conversion in the biblical meaning is more than a change of heart—an experience. It is an identification with a new people—the people of God whose history reaches back across the millenniums. We become part of the story of God's plan. As Peter writes in I Peter 2:10, we who were no people have become part of God's family. This family reaches back through two thousand years of history to the apostles and Jesus Christ, even to the prophets and the patriarchs. Today's church needs a sense of this continuity of history. Roots, if you please.

Within this larger family of God we need identity and a sense of who we are. We all have family roots, although we are members of the human race. Just so we as a Brethren in Christ denomination have roots and history that have made us what we are. The peril that rootlessness brings to a natural family is also present in a group of believers who disregard or even deny their roots. One of the weaknesses of our current evangelical scene is that our concern for the relevant and the individual has severed us from the past and our history. The current *independent* and *individual* emphasis is an unstable phenomenon.

As a church we have in the past taken our roots seriously. This 200th anniversary is an appropriate time to remind ourselves of not only Whose we are but who we are and in so doing to rediscover our identity.

No King but Caesar

The headline in Monday's (May 16, 1977) *South Bend Tribune* read, "Rhodesia Faces War from Zambia." The headline appeared justified by the content of the news release. It did not sound good.

Now, I know it is somewhat foolhardy to base an editorial on a news release. The situation can change rapidly and radically. Observations made at the time of the release may be obsolete by the time the editorial is read. Let it be clear that if the headline is not fulfilled we will all be grateful.

The headline did bring to my mind some very disquieting thoughts. Within each nation appearing in the headline there is the Brethren in Christ Church. I was present at the General Conference of 1973 when, because of the realities of the political situation, two General Conferences were organized—one in Rhodesia and one in Zambia.

To my knowledge, the Brethren in Christ have not in the past been citizens of both nations at war with each other. But the news release suggests that this could change and the hypothetical questions raised from time to time based on such possibility may no longer be hypothetical.

Realities such as the headlines suggest confirm the rightness of the traditional and doctrinal position of the Brethren in Christ in regards to the Christian's nonparticipation in war. Christians engaging in war against each other deny everything the Bible teaches about the church and the love Christians have for each other. They deny the oneness of the Body. They blaspheme our Lord's High Priestly prayer.

Now, this is not the first time that Christians have found themselves on opposite sides in a war. But it becomes somewhat more real when the situation involves those of our own fellowship. In each of the countries in the headline to which we referred are brethren and sisters we know and love. What is even more to the point is that they know each other. They have taken communion together. They have washed each other's feet. They serve the same Lord.

There are other biblical reasons for the Christian to refuse to take up the sword against his fellow man, but I know of none so compelling as a Christian's love for his fellow Christian regardless of national identity.

On the Worship of God

Recently I had the occasion to talk with a young man who during the past year has visited a large number of Brethren in Christ congregations. In our conversation he shared the observation—and his surprise—that in so many of these churches the United States flag was a part of the sanctuary furnishings. This confirmed an observation that I too had made.

The appearance of the national flag in our churches is a relatively recent phenomenon. It was not a part of the early meetinghouse furnishings. I believe that it has become a part of our worship symbols by two avenues.

In some instances the Brethren in Christ have taken over existing church buildings or provided pastoral leadership to a group whose roots were in another tradition. The national flag was a part of the sanctuary furnishings and continued to be after the change of ownership or leadership. The decision to retain the flag was not deliberate. The matter was not tested theologically. The flag was there; it just remained.

The flag may have found its way into the sanctuary by means of a gift or by a decision to make the decor more contemporary. It is very possible that the biblical or theological basis for the addition of this symbol to our worship was not the prime consideration. The practice of peer groups rather than biblical urgency dictated the change.

It would be appropriate to ask what the biblical basis of authority is for including the national flag as one of the symbols of worship. If it is not a symbol of worship or an aid to worship what is its purpose in the house of worship?

Symbols are powerful teaching instruments. Christ recognized this in instituting the Lord's Supper. The open Bible, the cross, the central pulpit, the communion table are symbols which quietly but effectively teach and aid in our worship.

Let me highlight biblical teachings which, I believe, bear upon the practice of including the national flag in our church furnishings.

Christ's teaching of the two kingdoms. At the beginning of his ministry Christ announced that "The Kingdom of God is at hand." At the close of his ministry he clearly stated that his kingdom was not of this world, else his disciples would have fought (John 18:36).

Are we not in danger of blurring Christ's teaching of the two kingdoms when we incorporate into our worship the symbol of the kingdom of this world? Even if we recognize the need for government and the biblical provision for it, one must admit that the values of the state are many times in radical opposition to the teachings of Christ. The church is a manifestation of this new kingdom with its own symbols—the cross, the Bible, the bread and the cup.

Separation of church and state. This principle is a concrete expression of the teaching concerning the two kingdoms. The state has its functions. The church has her mission. This principle of separation, which we take so much for granted, was purchased for us at great price. As Brethren in Christ, we are the direct descendants of those who paid by life and fortune for their understanding that the church and the state were separate.

I must ask if we are not betraying our heritage and those who suffered for this truth as we bring into our sanctuaries the high symbol of the state and seek to join what Christ has put asunder.

The transnational character of the church. Jesus was concerned about the activities in the house of God. He took some radical measures to correct the situation in the incident we refer to as "the cleansing of the Temple" (Mark 11:15-19). In the process he quoted Isaiah's statement, "My house shall be called a house of prayer for all the nations" (Isaiah 56:7).

Jesus affirmed a truth the Jews found difficult to accept; the house of God was for *all nations.* God is not a tribal deity nor a national god; nor is his church a national church. Do we not tamper with the biblical truth that the church of Jesus Christ is above nation and race when we include the national symbol among our worship symbols?

The teaching of peace and nonresistance. Symbols have a quiet but effective way of teaching. One could well ask the question what the presence of a national flag will do to our church's commitment to peace and nonresistance.

Obviously a national flag has other meaning than warfare. But it is so closely identified with the military that it is difficult to separate the two. I seriously question if our peace witness can long be maintained if each time the congregation gathers the nation's flag is part of the symbols in the sanctuary.

This relation of the flag to the military is symbolized frequently in most of our communities. It is in ours. The raising of the flag is a traditional part of our local high school's home football games. Just before the teams come onto the field the band moves into formation, the crowd faces the north end of the field, and a color guard from the local post of Veterans of Foreign Wars, armed with rifles, escorts the flag to the pole. The flag is raised to the playing of our national anthem with its distinct military overtones. I wonder if our youth seeing this relationship on Friday night can separate it on Sunday morning.

It is understandable that a government unit would find it appropriate to give prominence to the nation's symbol: our public schools are part of the state structure. The flag belongs over our post offices and government buildings. With this I have no problem.

The question which we as a church need to ask is this: Does the placing of the Stars and Stripes in the sanctuary contribute to the worship of God?

Wholeness

Recently I had conversation with one whose roots are several generations deep in the Brethren in Christ Church, but whose vocation has taken him and his family to where there is no Brethren in Christ congregation. This separation from the denomination led to inquiry about the church. He asked if I could in one word describe or characterize the church.

The occasion did not allow much time for reflection. The word I chose was somewhat spontaneous. I selected the word *wholeness*. I have had more time since our conversation to reflect on the question my friend asked and on my response. I have not yet come up with a better word.

I believe that the Brethren in Christ understanding of the Christian faith and the expression of this faith in life and mission justifies the choice of this term. There is a wholeness to the denomination's understanding of salvation, the human situation, and the church's mission.

The fall of man has numerous implications and manifestations. The Bible identifies these, among others, as death, guilt, alienation, enmity and bondage. The good news is that each expression of man's fall finds its antidote in God's grace. For man's guilt and disobedience there is forgiveness; for his enmity and alienation there is reconciliation; for his bondage there is redemption and deliverance; in his spiritual death there is new life, even life eternal.

The wholeness of salvation includes a change at the center of man's being where self has reigned supreme. The good news is that all of life can be brought into submission to Christ. In the resolution of this conflict one is no less a person. Rather, he is more truly a person when freed from the bondage of self to live in the glorious liberty which is in Christ.

This wholeness also includes seeing man as creature—a part of God's creation. He has physical needs; he is no ethereal being. He tires. He hungers. He bleeds. True to the teaching and ministry of Jesus, the Brethren in Christ recognize this part of man's nature. In obedience to Christ and as an expression of the love which we have experienced we reach out in love to our own and to our neighbor. We believe that true Christian faith feeds the hungry, clothes the naked, and warms the cold.

We are finite in our wisdom so we need the counsel of our fellow Christians. We are prone to failure and we need the reassurance of our brothers and sisters. We are susceptible to illness and need the prayers of the church as well as the care of the physician. We are a part of nature and are vulnerable to nature's cataclysms.

We not only need each other's assistance in times of trouble, we need each other at all times. The seventeenth-century preacher-poet, John Donne, said, "No man is an island entire of itself." Paul describes our interdependence as "members one of another." The meaning is clear. We are not meant to live out our pilgrimage alone. We need each other.

Written deep in Scripture and in the Brethren in Christ is this sense of community. The name itself speaks to this aspect of the Christian life. In a time when community is disintegrating and the family is under stress, when mobility and separation bring their own kinds of isolation and loneliness for many, the church becomes the stable and supportive community.

This wholeness is also well expressed in a dual concern to be God's people and to do God's work. A concern for the health of the body is balanced by a concern for the mission of the church. The health of the body is seen in a commitment to truth and righteousness—doctrine and life. This concern, unless balanced by ministry, can lead to introspection and to nurturing spiritual hypochondriacs. Ministry, unless balanced by truth and piety, can lead to humanitarian do-goodism and paternalism.

No theological system is perfect, no biblical interpretation without some blind spots. We still know only in part. But we commend the Brethren in Christ understanding of the Christian faith to long-term members of the church and prospective members alike. We believe that there is a wholeness in this understanding that brings the fullness of the Christian faith to the broad spectrum of man's need and in doing so is able to create whole persons.

Brethren in Christ Weather

It may be my age.

It may be because the quiet and secure town of Nappanee was for the first time out of gas for several days last month.

It may be because Salt II which promised so much appears to have produced so little.

Or perhaps I am reading the wrong newspapers, watching the

wrong networks, or subscribing to the wrong magazines.

But I am beginning to believe that Chicken Little was right—the sky is falling.

This, I believe, is Brethren in Christ weather.

I believe that a correct reading of the signs of the times indicates the decline of western culture. The age of economic abundance is coming to a close. A loss of purpose and a lack of moral undergirding is undermining our political life. The center of gravity for the Christian faith will shift to Third World countries. Along with this shift the light and salt will disappear from western cultures.

Christian presuppositions which have undergirded our institutions and community life are already disappearing. We will find less and less support for moral and ethical standards in our laws and in our customs.

The closing decades of the twentieth century will not be easy years for the west. Nor will these decades be easy for nominal Christianity. But these decades will offer a unique opportunity for those churches who find in the New Testament the pattern for their new life in Christ and their life together.

The Brethren in Christ have the potential to be such a church.

We are a believers' church. When we get behind the words to the meaning of a "believers' church" we are speaking of a church in which membership is based on a first-hand faith—a personal and responsible decision to follow Christ.

This is in contrast to a second-hand faith—a birthright faith—by which one sort of automatically becomes a part of the Christian community. When church membership is no longer the expected and popular position in a community, a second-hand faith will not be sufficient.

It will need to be a first-hand faith to stand.

We have an understanding of the tension between the world and the Christian life. Writ deep in our history is the biblical teaching of the peril of the world. If we take seriously this understanding of the world, we will be the better prepared theologically when the tension becomes greater.

As our structures disintegrate, freedom will be curtailed. The more secular our society becomes the greater the pressures on those with Christian conscience. This should come as no surprise to us. In our own history and especially in our Anabaptist roots the world was an ever-present danger.

It is our present task to define the world that is this peril in order that we are not charmed by it in the present age nor taken by surprise in the years to come.

We have a heritage of costly discipleship. We find it in our roots.

Men and women paid for their faith with their lives. Those who were not martyred were aware of the possibility of their dying for their faith.

I recently stood by the grave of Ulrich Engle, the father of Jacob Engle, identified as a leader in the founding group of the Brethren in Christ. I was reminded again that he and others were part of a band who left Switzerland to accept the promise of religious freedom offered by William Penn.

Incorporated in the early confessions and included in teaching and preaching was the concept of costly discipleship. We may miss an element of joy in that early preaching and teaching; our fathers would no doubt miss the seriousness in ours. Their teaching reflected Jesus' command to count the cost before beginning a building, or engaging in a war, or following him.

Such teaching has a way of producing "all-weather" Christians.

We have a sense of community. Experience and teaching were not sufficient for our fathers. In this they were reading the New Testament correctly. There needs to be a community to support one another. This community is identified by love and caring in our life together, and by a sense of destiny in the life to come.

As society's structures disintegrate and the fabric of our culture comes apart, the sense of community in our society will fade. Hurts will not be healed. Fears will multiply, suspicion and mistrust increase. There will be no balm to heal.

In this social wasteland the Christian church, if it is truly a loving and faithful community, will be a refuge and an oasis. This concept is not foreign to us as a church. Like our concept of discipleship and our understanding of the world, it has remained residual in our life and doctrine—recognized at times more in lip-service than in practice. But it is there.

These elements—a first-hand faith, an awareness of the world, costly discipleship, and a sense of community—are essential elements in the faith that will survive in stormy weather.

We may not look with anticipation to the weather ahead, but I believe that it is weather for which the Brethren in Christ are prepared by heritage and doctrine.

The Gospel We Preach

Fellowship is important to us. Whether it is a 200th Anniversary Conference or a small retreat, we enjoy being together. This is reflected as well in testimonies new members give of their experience in our local congregations. This emphasis on brotherhood is historical; it is biblical; it is Brethren in Christ.

We have some gift for administration. Our administration pattern may not be perfect but in light of my contacts I would not trade our organization for any I know. We think it can be improved. So we are at work church-wide on taking a new look at our structure, our resources, and our use of these resources.

Theology and doctrine do not receive the same priority in our expenditure of time and funds as do these areas we have just referred to. We are not as comfortable in doing theology as we are in devising structure or fostering fellowship or planning programs.

We dare not neglect the area of theology any longer. When we were a homogeneous group (in the days before the radio ministers and the television churches) we could assume that we knew what we believed and that it was generally believed among us.

This is no longer true. There is increasing doctrinal and experiential diversity among us. The doctrinal section of the manual is variously interpreted or piously ignored. We may have consensus on the least common denominator of Christian truth, but we do not have consensus on a theology that will create a high sense of commitment to and pride in the denomination.

When we have taken a good look at our structure and funding we should turn our efforts with all deliberate speed to doctrine and theology. If we are to have respect for the doctrinal section of our manual we will either need to bring it in line with where we are as a church or call for a renewed commitment to it as it now stands.

But before we begin revising our doctrine we have much theological homework to do. It is urgent that the General Conference takes steps to foster a study of theological and biblical truth as it has taken steps to study structure, to foster fellowship, and to promote program.

Doctrinal statements cannot be written on the floor of the General Conference. These must come out of the life of the church as scholars, teachers, pastors, and the rest of us gather together around the Word and in honesty and obedience listen to the Spirit and to each other.

The time is here for the church to give attention to a study of cardinal doctrines and theological issues—Christian experience (including conversion and sanctification), the interpretation of the Bible, the meaning of the world and the Christian's relation to it, the Christian and the state, the doctrine of the last things, the church and the ministry, and God's sovereignty and man's freedom, to name a few.

Some of these are more pertinent than others, both in interest and in substance. But each of them represents substantial diversity of understanding within the church.

This is not a call for rigid doctrinaire conformity. It is a call for us as a church to discover what is our understanding of the gospel which we preach and teach. We may well be prepared to allow for varying degrees of deviation but at least we will know what is deviation.

Part 3
Editorials
for the
Church at Large

Lantern in the Dawn

A MEDITATION ON JOHN 1:1-18

My early years were spent on a Kansas dairy farm. Still in my memory are those dark and often cold winter mornings when my father would announce that it was time to rise and be about the morning chores.

Those were the days before rural electrification had arrived in our area of Kansas. So in the darkness we would light a kerosene lantern and by its light find our way to the barn. In the barn there were nails and hooks from which to hang the lantern as we went about the morning tasks. As the location of our tasks shifted we would take the lantern with us and continue to work from its feeble light.

As we proceeded with our work, if we took the time to look, we could notice in the east a faint grayish light along the wide Kansas horizon. Slowly this grayish color would move further up the sky and the east would take on a reddish glow, and then slowly a bright red or orange ball would push up over the horizon. The night was gone. The day had come.

While this was all going on, usually quite unnoticed, the lantern continued to hang there giving forth its light. Finally we would be aware that no longer were we being guided by the lantern, for its light was now scarcely seen in the brilliance of the dawn.

In John 5:35 Jesus made a similar observation when he, speaking to the Jews concerning John, said, "He (John the Baptist) was a burning and shining lamp and you were willing to rejoice for a while in his light." But now a greater than John was present—this "burning and shining light" had given way to the dawn—Jesus had now come.

The writer of the fourth Gospel has the same imagery in mind when he writes "In him was life and the life was the light of men. The light shines in the darkness and the darkness has not overcome it."

These statements are taken from John's account of the Incarnation: "In the beginning was the Word, and the Word was with

71

God, and the Word was God—and the Word became flesh and dwelt among us, full of grace and truth."

The lanterns of old have been superseded by the dawn. They served the predawn hours admirably but now the "dayspring from on High has visited us." Why walk around with a lantern when the sun has appeared?

There was the lantern of natural revelation. Paul refers to it in Romans 1. God can be seen in his creation. The incredible size of the universe, the dependability of its laws, the mystery of the atom, the complexity of the human nervous system, and the phenomenon of nature give us intimations of a divine power we call God.

As persuasive as are the "starry heavens above," so also is the moral law within. Man's sense of ought and his desire for meaning and belonging find their counterpart in man's sense of guilt and loneliness and meaninglessness. From societies primitive to societies sophisticated this image of God, written upon man's nature, finds expression in varied religious forms—worship, sacrifices, myths, idols, and deities.

This tells us something about God's power and design and his moral nature, but it is just a lantern. Its light is limited, the revelation incomplete, and the reality it suggests shadowy and distorted.

But we have a better lamp—that of special revelation—through the Old Testament Scriptures.

God is revealed in his mighty acts in the Old Testament. The calling of a people, the forming of a nation, their deliverance from Egypt, the giving of the Law at Sinai with thunder and lightning and awesome manifestations. God had spoken and acted definitely in time and in history, but this was only a lantern. "For the law was given through Moses; grace and truth came through Jesus Christ."

Light came through the prophets with their call to inwardness and their warning against trusting in ritual and form. Hear Isaiah's call to repentance or Micah's moving answer to the question of what God requires: ". . . to do justly, and to love mercy, and to walk humbly with thy God."

It is not too strong to state that in the days of the prophets the eastern sky was beginning to become light. Indeed a crimson glow could at times be seen as when Jeremiah speaks of the new covenant written upon the heart or when Isaiah breaks forth with the vision of the Suffering Servant. Those were great souls and great visions. But they were walking with a lantern.

But when the dawn came, "The true light that lighteth every

man was coming into the world." "A light for revelation to the Gentiles and for glory to thy people Israel." It is not without basis that Isaiah's great hymn is seen as Messianic. "The people that walked in darkness have seen a great light. "They that dwell in the land of the shadow of death, upon them has the light shined." The Incarnation means that the night is over. Put away your lanterns—smoky, dim, and flickering—for the dawn has come. The day is here. The sun of righteousness has arisen. This must mean that in Jesus Christ we can see God and reality—not partially, not in types and shadows but in truth. "No one has ever seen God; the only son, who is in the bosom of the Father, he has made him known." Hear Jesus in his own words to Philip: "He who has seen me has seen the Father," or the writer to the Hebrews when he describes Christ as bearing "the very stamp of his (God's) nature."

Mankind who had lived by lanterns—some smoky and flickering, others bright and brilliant, but still only a lantern—now had the sun. The Son, John says, reflects God's glory. "We have beheld his glory, glory as of the only son of God. And so we ask, "What was so glorious about the Incarnation?"

The Incarnation reveals God's glory in his provision for man's deep need. In Christ the law and the prophets were fulfilled. The rituals of the Old Testament were made real in his death and resurrection. The face of God was seen more clearly. It was the face of Grace and revealed the countenance of a father, "for as many as received him (Christ) to them gave he power to become the sons of God."

The Incarnation reveals God's glory in his attitude towards the common, the simple, and the weak. Who of us would have written the story of the Incarnation as God acted it out on the stage of history? Two weary and worn travelers, the woman obviously heavy with child; a "no vacancy" sign at the inn, a cave as shelter for the night and as the delivery room for the birth, a manger as the crib and shepherds the first curious visitors. This first scene set the tone for the entire drama of his life. The years of his preparation and the years of his ministry were as well marked by the absence of power and pomp and prestige.

No Horatio Alger story this. No rags to riches. No log cabin to the White House. His destiny was a Roman cross in the presence of a curious and taunting crowd.

This seems so strange because we have understood glory in the terms of lanterns. Power and wealth and armies and splendor and magnitude and dominance. The dawn reveals God's understanding of glory: hands laid upon a leper, fingers placed on the eyes of the blind, children gathered up in his arms, words of forgiveness to a woman caught in an adulterous act, the noticing of the widow's two mites, and the alabaster box broken and its ointment mingled with tears of a forgiven sinner. Are we not expected to see the glory of God in the upper room when the Incarnate Son took a towel, bound it around his waist and washed his disciples' feet—the glory of a servant role?

We say this was his humiliation. John did not say that. He said this was "his glory, glory as of the only Son from the Father." Paul wrote, "(God) has shone in our hearts to give the knowledge of the glory of God in the face of Jesus Christ."

All of this says something about our values and our methods and our witness. It says something about our understanding of Scripture and doctrine and morals and ethics. Is our understanding of God and his dealing with men based on lanterns or on the dawn?

There is nothing quite so important as a man's concept of God. If his concept is inadequate or distorted, sincerity and devotion compounds the error and makes him worse rather than better. How essential it is that our understanding is based upon God as revealed by his Son in whose dawning the light of the lanterns becomes very dim indeed.

Playing It Safe

MATTHEW 25:14-30

I read again the Parable of the Talents. I confess some sympathy for that poor fellow with the one talent.

He may not have been very proud of what he had done, but certainly he did not expect to receive what he got. Surely prudence is a virtue and warrants commendation. A note of caution is always in order. A man could lose everything, he reasoned. So he played it safe.

Poor man! "You wicked and slothful servant . . . take the talent from him . . . cast . . . into outer darkness . . ." Judgment could hardly have been more severe had he lost the talent.

If I read this parable correctly, it seems to say that faithful stewardship involves risk. To play it safe is a betrayal of the steward's role. It seems that there is a divine law which decrees that those who live by fear rather than by faith will lose it all and God will bypass them as he uses others.

How often do we re-enact the role of the man with the one talent? Fearful of failure and comfortable in the status quo, we live by caution rather than by faith. We play it safe rather than risk it all. Old and tried solutions are offered to new problems. Formalized answers are given to radical and earnest questions.

I know of no right course that is not without risk. If it does not involve risk, be assured that it is the wrong course. It would be much safer to keep the six-year old at home rather than send him off to school. Much safer to keep the son on the farm than to allow him to go to college. Much safer to remain single than to run the risk of marriage. Much safer to remain childless than to assume the responsibilities of parenthood.

Just as it is with the individual, so is it with the church. The right and proper course is the one with risk. If the church is to be faithful in her ministry, she dare not play it safe. The church at Jerusalem wanted to play it safe and to make the Gentiles enter the church by a tried and sure pattern. The Roman Church wanted to play it safe. She feared the results when each man would be his own priest and his own interpreter of God's word. What looseness of morals and ethics would result if a man was justified by faith alone! There have been times since the days of Martin Luther when caution replaced faith and the church decided to play it safe. This danger is ever with us.

The church is today face to face with a culture radically different from that of a generation ago. The materialistic and the sensual confront us through all of the media. Youth and adults are far more sophisticated and knowledgeable. The explosion of knowledge and our scientific accomplishments have captured our faith and have become our religion. The shorter work week and the affluence of our society empty our communities for many weekends and even weeks of the year.

One in every four homes has a history of divorce. Forces economic and social pull at the very fabric of our homes. Many are seeking release from a meaningless life through drugs or religious movements. The mobility of our population destroys the sense of community. The urbanization of our society multiplies problems social and personal.

In face of these radical and rapid changes it is my concern that the church does not bury her head in the sands of yesterday and appease her conscience with busy work. These radical problems call for radical faith. Never has the gospel been more needed. Never

have the implications of this gospel been more relevant. This is
not a call for a new gospel. It is a call for radical faith. It is not to
advocate that we throw caution to the wind. It is a plea that we do
not steer by it.

Let each of us search our own souls. Better still, let us call upon
God to search us and to do a great thing for us and through us. May
we ever remember that it is a paradox of the Kingdom that he who
plays it safe will hear the words of judgement and will lose even
that which he seeks to preserve.

" 'Specially Me, Lord!"

It was some little time ago. A number of us—five or six—met for
a time of sharing and praying. We shared concerns and needs and
took our turn in praying. One of the group, as he prayed, concluded his petitions by the phrase " 'Specially me, Lord!"

This kind of praying gets through. One recalls the prayer that
came out of China in the early decades of our century, "Lord,
revive Thy Church, and begin it with Me." Or the haunting
refrain of the Negro Spiritual:

> "It's not my brother, nor my sister,
> But it's me, O Lord,
> Standin' in the need of prayer."

As we examine each area of our lives and the relationships that
make it up, and as we seek God's help and grace in these relationships and pray for those about us, it may not be inappropriate to
make these words a part of our prayers—" 'Specially me, Lord!"

There is the home and the family. The pressure of schedules.
The span of different ages. The diversity of interests. The friction
of personalities. The taking of each other for granted. The forces
which would destroy the home. These are a part of the average
home. Nowhere are we more transparent! Nowhere is the reality or
sham of our faith more apparent! In no area of our life is prayer
more important. And as we pray, let us say, " 'Specially me,
Lord!"

Then there is the place where we work, eight or more hours a
day, five or six days a week. There is the unreasonable customer.

The inconsiderate employer. The irresponsible employee. The phone that rings incessantly. The girl at the next desk who either never talks or never stops. The fellow employee who is after our job. The routine that just about has us down. God has grace for the office or the factory or the store and wants us to bring to him these problems and these personalities and as we pray, say, " 'Specially me, Lord!"

And then there is the life of the church. It is here where so much that is important hinges. Here is where spiritual resources should be available. Here our youth should find answers to vital questions. Here fellowship should be found. Here burdens shared. Here hearts should find peace and joy. This is not always the case. The program drags. Some are loaded with work, others do nothing except criticize, and tensions exist where harmony is expected. The public services lack something. We know that what we need is a visitation of the Spirit, a revival of devotion to God and of love for his people. And so we pray. But as we pray, may we say, " 'Specially me, Lord!"

I recall the statement of one of our respected churchmen with wide experience as an evangelist. He said that in his early ministry he assumed that in order to have a moving of God in the community and among the non-Christians it was necessary for all the church members to get right with God and their brethren. However, he found through experience that as desirable as this would be, it was not necessary. What was necessary was for three or four of the members to meet this conditon and take upon their hearts the needs of the congregation and community. Then God would begin to work. Is not this what Jesus meant when he said "If two of you shall agree . . ." or "Where two or three are gathered together . . ."

To those of us who are deeply concerned, let us continue in prayer that there will be a visitation of God upon his Church.

And as we pray, say, " 'Specially me, Lord!"

In Defense of Optimism

MATTHEW 16:18

It is not easy to be an optimist these days. Even the word itself is in disrepute. To suggest that one is an optimist is to raise questions as to his judgment and even as to his theology.

It would be repetitious to list the conditions and events that form the basis for pessimism. From the mass media as well as the sophisticated, the secular as well as the religious press, the theme is somber and the colors dark. To escape the stigma that is associated with pessimism, those who share this mood justify their positions by claiming to be realists.

Now, the church has every reason to be realistic. She is aware that the problems of our society are deeper than solutions widely offered. She is aware that no amount of money appropriated, no increase in knowledge and education, no multiplicity of laws will in themselves meet the real need of men and the problems of our society. It is easy for the church to lose heart. There is the temptation to withdraw within her pietistic refuge or to wait passively for her Lord's return.

Indeed Christian realism tells us that the patient's condition is worse than most people believe. The self-centeredness of man and his pride result in his disobedience and arrogance toward God and his fear and hatred of his fellow men. Unless these causes of man's problems are reckoned with, the patient will grow worse. Indeed it is a "sickness unto death." The church should know this and needs to be realistic about it.

If the church's realism is cause for pessimism, it is also the basis for optimism. Read again Peter's confession (Matthew 16:16) and Christ's reply (Matthew 16:18, 19). Too often this response of Jesus has been interpreted as the church's assurance of preservation in spite of the attacks of the forces of hell.

Read it again! The meaning is quite the opposite. It is hell that is under attack. Hell's gates shall be battered down. The church is on the march and "the gates of hell shall not withstand her." The church's victory is assured.

Nor are all the signs of the times cause for despair. The restlessness of youth is not necessarily reason for despair. It may well be a basis for hope. For an increasing number of our youth a house in the suburbs, a respectable job, a secure retirement, and other marks of material and social success are not enough. They are unwilling to sell their birthright for a mess of pottage. Their quest takes on some strange and disturbing expressions. However, if we had the insight and understanding of Christ, I wonder if we would not say that they are not far from the kingdom—indeed closer than are their parents.

In the breakdown of community due to urbanization and the mobility of our society, there is a new opportunity for the church to supply this sense of community—indeed the true community which exists where men have been reconciled to God and to one another. The individual's life has become impersonal. His job is determined by the union or taken by automation. He no longer goes to a doctor but to a clinic. His life from birth to death is computerized. This means that man feels lost and helpless with nowhere to turn and with no one to listen.

How relevant for our times is the message of God's love for the individual and of his forgiveness for the guilty! How relevant for our day is the fellowship of those who love, and care, and listen.

Could it be that our despair and pessimism are because we look at the church as *our* church when she is really *his* church and he is her head. We need to see man's needs as Christ sees them. We must assign priorities as he assigns them. We must measure success as he measures it. Our methods must be subject to his judgment. We must become the channel through which the supernatural power of the Holy Spirit can flow.

We would not be faithful to the New Testament if we did not recognize that the way to life is through death and that the redemptive ministry is identified with suffering. Our optimism is not contingent upon a future in which the church is respectable and popular. Our optimism is contingent upon a church directed and motivated by him who is her Lord—a terror to evil but a refuge for the sinner. ". . . terrible as an army with banners," but also a household of faith where love is supreme. We also must see that over all shines the the promise of a New Age as Christ returns at the end of time.

The opportunities are legion. The Gospel is adequate. As pastors and laymen, churchmen and missionaries, parents and teachers, we need to recapture the mood of the New Testament and hear the words of the Lord when he said, "All power is given unto me in heaven and earth . . ." And again as he said, ". . . I will build my church and the gates of hell shall not prevail against it."

Both in the temper of our times and in the nature of his church there is real basis for optimism.

Just One Generation Away

If the church is to continue, each generation needs to experience a personal encounter with Christ and a personal commitment to him. This is why evangelism is a continuous obligation. This is why Christian nurture must be constantly pursued. Although the eternal quality of the church is assured from the viewpoint of God's power and grace, from the human aspect the church is always just one generation away from extinction.

Now, this is the reason our ministry to youth is so important. We dare not be satisfied if they have only a nominal and emotional loyalty to the church and the Christian faith. It is necessary that youth experience a life changing encounter with God and that this experience finds expression in a life of discipleship and fellowship. Only in this way will there be a church tomorrow.

We have had an emphasis within our church of home nurture and childhood conversions. The benefits of such an emphasis are many. However, there is an ever present danger. It is that the religious experience of childhood may not be the New Testament concept of conversion marked by repentance and faith. The result is a vague understanding of conversion, a birthright Christian instead of a committed disciple.

If we are to have a vital church tomorrow, it is imperative that parents and teachers, pastors and church leaders have an understanding of both the values and the limitations of childhood conversions. In our theology and our practice we need to make provisions for a meaningful decision made at a responsible age with mature understanding.

In addition to a recognition of the crucial problem just mentioned, we need to be aware of the importance of our attitude towards youth and their questions.

We need to be *honest* with them. They have real questions. We should deal with these questions with integrity. They have every right to raise these questions. There has been a wide gap between Christian claims and realization; there have been dogmas which retreated in the face of increased knowledge; there have been wide discrepancies between the proclamation of Christian love and its expression by the church. The answers to these questions are not easy.

The relation of psychology to Christian experience; the age of the earth and Genesis; the fact of space travel, organ transplants, thought control, and genetic planning have tremendous implications for our faith. A reservoir of scripture texts, a period of prayer, and a "God Bless You" will not be sufficient. We will ignore these questions at our peril. These are "for real" and demand our attention and honest answers.

Our ministry to youth demands *competency*. Not every Sunday school teacher or youth leader may match the educational qualities of the high school teacher. However, it is possible and indeed

necessary that each congregation place at the disposal of our youth
the highest committed competence available. It may well mean
that the ministry of those outside the congregation will need to be
called upon from time to time.

In the years of senior high and college life, determining decisions are made—occupations, marriage, military service, and life
values. We owe it to our youth to assist them in making these life
decisions with honesty and concern but also with competence. We
expect competence when we take our car to the garage, our children to the public school, or ourselves to the clinic. In none of
these situations is sincerity a substitute for competency. Neither is
it within the church.

Finally, youth is entitled to come face to face with Christians
who are *committed*. I do not anticipate that we will be able to
answer all their questions. Nor do I envision that every local
congregation can match the training and competence of our high
schools and colleges. There is however, a unique quality within
the church for which we should not need to make excuse. This is
the reality of a committed life. The power of real Christian commitment is such that it will either convince youth to the point of
commitment or else haunt them through the wasteland of their
lives if they refuse the call of Christ.

It seems to me that youth may very well expect to find within the
present generation living examples of what it really means to be a
Christian—lives that are motivated by an inner experience of
God's grace, lives that are characterized by understanding and
compassion, lives that give concrete expression to suffering and
redemptive love, lives that are marked by a great certainty, lives
that dare to be transparent because of an awareness of God's
forgiveness and his power.

If the church cannot provide such examples, maybe we should
just forget the whole matter. It will hardly be worth our effort or
our youth's time.

The ultimate responsibility for the next generation resides with
the home. Our homes are in need of help. Many are the parents
who have taken time from the life of the home to give to the
church—time which they could ill-afford to give. It was given
because they believed that the church should be and would be a
source of aid in the responsibilities of the home and in their hour
of need.

Now is just such an hour. We are just one generation away . . .

The Two Commandments

Our nation and society are in deep trouble. One of the obvious manifestations of this crisis is racial tension with its threat of violence.

The solutions offered—jobs, education, housing, justice, and equality of opportunity—will require the efforts and cooperation of all sectors of our society. Government, business, and education are all involved. In an hour such as this we do well to ask, "What is the Christian's role?

Several observations as to the evangelical responsibility may be in order.

The Christian and the Christian church need to be on the side of human rights. Christian love requires it. The future of missions to non-white and non-western peoples depends upon it. We may not agree on the expression this concern may take—and surely Christian ends do not justify un-Christian means—but our hearts must be touched and indeed moved by the indignities and the injustice which have been the lot of the Negro in our midst. When we are disturbed by the lawlessness and violence which erupts from the ghettos—as indeed we should be—let us be equally vocal in our concern for the conditions which breed desperation and disrespect for law.

Our individual witness should be on the side of human rights. The conversation in our homes and the reaction to other racial groups in our community should reflect respect and Christian love. Statements of intolerance and prejudice and disrespect may at times need to be countered with the word of understanding and love.

We need to understand that Christ gave his approval to two commandments:

"Thou shalt love the Lord thy God . . ."
"Thou shalt love thy neighbor as thyself"

As evangelicals we have been rightly concerned with obedience to the first. There is justification in granting to it priority. There is however a second commandment. Too long we have understood the fulfillment of this in the terms of "charity." We have failed to take seriously the term "as thyself." There are occasions where charity and benevolence are high expressions of Christian love. But when the test of "as thyself" is put to Christian love, it must go beyond "charity." To love our neighbor as ourselves is to desire for him what we desire for ourselves, and for his children what we desire for our own.

This love needs to find concrete expression—must be incarnate—in a ministry. We can be overwhelmed by the magnitude and difficulty of the task. However, there *must be something* we can do in face of such great need. There need to be efforts at understanding, lifting, sharing, loving, and reconciling which will enhance dignity, encourage responsibility, and kindle hope. The church needs to assist those who have the opportunity to become first class citizens to assume the responsibilities which this brings, to experience the spiritual life which undergirds these responsibilities, and to place spiritual and eternal values in proper perspective.

We need to recognize as well that when all the laws have been passed, all the necessary funds appropriated, and all the cities rebuilt, hatred and prejudice will be present still. Centuries of oppression and injustice have taken their toll in the character of those who have been victims of this oppression. It is to these spiritual and moral needs, which no amount of laws passed or funds appropriated can reach, that the church has a unique responsibility in this period of revolution.

There is both the message and the ministry of reconciliation. It is doubtful that they will listen to the message unless they have seen and felt the ministry. It is even more doubtful that we can be true to our ministry if we fail to share the message of God's transforming grace.

A Christian Christian

EPHESIANS 6

Joseph T. Bayly suggests that there is a subtle difference between being a Christian and being Christian. I was intrigued with the suggestion. The idea would not go away.

Is there not the very real possibility that one may be a Christian but not be Christian? Indeed, do not we know some non-Christians who are more Christian than some Christians whom we know? Is it not the great purpose of Christian nurture to make Christians Christian?

"And he gave some apostles . . . for the perfecting of the saints . . . till we all come . . . unto the measure of the stature of the fullness of Christ."

In the latter portion of the sixth chapter of Ephesians the Apostle Paul describes what is involved in a Christian being Christian.

In verse 25 he states that Christians should be Christian in business dealings and neighbor relations. Christian ethics rather than demands are the measure. The Golden Rule and love for the neighbor are the plumbline of their dealings. Honesty and fairness are the characteristics.

Have you dealt with Christians and were not certain that everything was really open and above board? Have you known Christains who used questionable means to obtain their ends? I submit that if these Christians had been Christian, these dealings would have been far different.

According to verse 28 Christians should be Christian in their work. This relates to what we work, how we work, and why we work. For a Christian a *good* job is not measured solely by size of salary, opportunity for advancement, or ease of task. A *good* job is measured by the good a job produces. There is as well the Christian way for an employee to work. A little more effort than is demanded, a little more care than is required, a second mile attitude towards fellow employees, and willingness to do the menial are the marks of Christian work and often determine if one is a Christian Christian.

Our attitudes toward others (verse 31) can be the difference between being a Christian or Christian. Attitudes that are critical, malicious, judgmental, and harsh are not Christian. The words chosen and the inflection used, as well as the questions asked and the look in the eyes, reveal the heart. To be Christian calls for understanding, tolerance, sympathy, and generosity. These are the marks of a Christian Christian.

There needs to be the quality of compassion and courtesy (verse 32). The gracious attitude which is so often lacking among Christians is so necessary if one is to be Christian. Consideration of others and the willingness to give of one's time and self are qualities of Christian character as essential as are honesty and morality. So often when I listen to conservatives—theological and political—I am impressed with their logic but disturbed by their lack of compassion. What the times need are not only orthodoxy of the head but also orthodoxy of the heart—not only more Christians but men and women who are more Christian.

The little child said it simply and non-theologically when he prayed "Dear God, make the bad people good and the good people nice." He wanted to see some Christian Christians.

The Forgotten Word

It is not only a forgotten word. It is almost a naughty word. The word is *ought*.

It is forgotten because we use it so seldom in respect to our own actions. It survives primarily as we use it in reference to others.

It is a naughty word because we expect actions to result from inward motivations which cause "want to" to replace "ought to." So, if we must call upon "ought" to determine our actions, we have serious questions about our inner motivation or the worthiness of the object of our action.

Within the past year I heard a speaker expressing with evangelistic zeal the concept of proper motivation in industry. The efficiency and success of an industry is crucially dependent upon proper motivation. Production could be increased and the morale of all employees raised by inner motivation. A "want to" would replace "ought to."

It is the same in the classroom. Learning is not to be seen as a rigorous discipline to be pursued, but an exciting adventure in which one is caught up. If in the course of his education less than acceptable work is performed by the student, a proper and understandable reason is "I just don't like that subject" or "That teacher doesn't turn me on." In other words, motivation is lacking.

This same philosophy has crept into Christian living, especially where there is a strong emphasis upon experience. It is suggested that experience will provide the inner motivation by which a "want to" will replace "ought to." The logic goes something like this: There are four stages of human behavior.

First—and at the bottom—are those who do as they jolly well please. No moral restraint conditions their actions. Totally self-centered, only legal restraint, social pressure, or the inability to realize their desire prevents them.

Second, is that group who know that they should live by certain standards and values, and indeed desire to do so. They find, however, the struggle too intense. The words of the Apostle Paul ". . . for what I would, that do I not; but what I hate, that do I," is the picture of their lives.

Third, are those who have found strength and grace to realize the "ought." The "want to" however is "double minded" since there is the wish to fulfill the *ought* as well as the *want*. The desire of the self is present with the desire to serve God. Even in the face of this tension the *ought* is often victor over the *want*.

The fourth—and highest—stage is the completion of the cycle. We are again back to where we do again as we want. Only now we want to do what we ought—and are able to do it. The phrase "Love God and do as you please" states the principle rather boldly.

I should explain that I have oversimplified the subject and that I am not opposed to motivation either in the factory, classroom, or church. I should hasten to add that I believe in the reality of the "fourth state of grace" where our deep subconscious desires are brought into subjection to Christ and our love for him causes us to want to do his will.

But no business succeeds when each person's performance is based upon "want to," no matter how high the motivation. Success in a profession is both a rigorous discipline and a high adventure. No marriage, however fervent the motivation, will be what it is meant to be if the word "ought" is missing from the vocabulary of each party as it applies to his or her own life. No missionary effort succeeds without the "ought" in it.

There will never be real Christian maturity when the "ought" is missing. No spiritual tide of a church will rise high enough and no program will be vital enough so that the "ought" can be dropped from the vocabulary of the members' responsibilities.

Christian living is a marriage of motivation and obligation, a combination of "want to" and "ought to." I find this in the Gospels. There never was a question of our Lord's desire to do his Father's will. But there were incidents in his life when the "ought to" shone through. The writer of the Fourth Gospel refers to Christ's journey from Judea to Galilee and states "He must needs go through Samaria." Jesus told the Pharisees: "these ought ye to have done, and not to leave the others undone." He told the disciples that men "ought always to pray." The garden scene is the supreme example when his action was determined not by what he wanted but what God wanted.

Ours is a time when permissiveness is the description of our moral climate and happiness and comfort the essence of so much that passes for Christian faith. In this context it is urgent that we bear witness to New Testament discipleship by restoring the "ought" to the Christian vocabulary.

Morality and Horsepower

Billy* would have been a sophomore this year in the local high school. But Billy was not present for the opening of school. He had been killed in an automobile accident at a culvert on a country road five weeks before school was to open.

Donna* might well have been the Homecoming Queen. But Donna, an only daughter, was not even a candidate. She had died two weeks before the homecoming game as a result of a crash at a rural crossroad.

These two deaths are only two of tens of thousands which are expected to occur on our highways this year—more deaths than suffered by our country in the first World War and twice as many as in the seven-year conflict in Viet Nam. We may be almost as safe on the streets of our inner cities as on the highways of our nation. There is a murder committed every forty-three minutes; there is a highway death every ten.

Has not this loss of life taken on moral proportions? Is it not time that the church calls irresponsible driving sin? Has not the time come when it is as morally wrong to disregard a traffic law as it is to cheat on your income tax returns? Have we not reached the point where it becomes the church's obligation to speak out on the Christian implications of driving?

The Christian's respect for law and authority should include traffic laws. Our youth will hardly have more respect for law than their parents. For too many of us the game of "cops and driver" has the same fascination that "cops and robbers" has for another segment of our society. Let us not waste our sympathy on the driver whom we see stopped along the highway with a red light flashing behind him. We who are gratified that the bank in which we have our money is safeguarded by a secret alarm system should be equally enthused about radar which protects our lives on our highways.

Our respect for law should not be determined by the presence or absence of law enforcement officers. We have long believed and taught that sin consists of the breaking of a law and not in being caught.

As Christians we know that "no man liveth unto himself." We are influencing behavior by our example. There seems little excuse to encourage youth's latent obsession with power and speed by our own example and boasting. It is high time that we stop bragging about how fast we made the trip. It is also high time to impress our youth that life is more than bucket seats and "four on the floor."

Driving is a full time job. Your life—even more the lives of those with you—and the thousands you meet (with a six foot space between) are in your hands when you take the wheel. This is no time to plan your sales strategy or solve your personnel problems. This is not the time to outline your Sunday sermon. This is neither the time to settle arguments nor to be overly affectionate. There is too much at stake to be either casual or distracted when one drives.

The grounds for Christian responsibility is found in both Testaments. In the haunting question asked in the dawn of human history, "Am I my brother's keeper?" and the high standard demanded by Christ to "love thy neighbor as thyself," we find the basis of Christian conduct behind the wheel.

Driving has become a moral issue. As Christians and as the church we need to develop a driving conscience.

These are their real names.

Living a Questionable Life

I PETER 3:15

Books are written on the subject. Sermons are preached on it. Classes are held on technique. We know we ought to do it. We feel guilty if we don't.

I am talking about witnessing.

So we finally screw up our courage. Try to find the right time or bring the conversation to the appropriate point and then we witness. A little forced perhaps. Didn't quite come out as we had planned. Our conscience is appeased. But we are not quite certain that this is what Jesus meant when he said "Ye shall be witnesses . . ."

Maybe there would be some help for us if we turned to the setting from which this imagery is taken. It is a courtroom. We are the witnesses. We are not the judge—although there is the temptation. We are not the prosecuting attorney—although much of what passes for witnessing takes on this aspect. We are the witnesses—to tell what we know from first hand knowledge.

Take a brief look at the classical example of person to person witnessing—Jesus with the Samaritan woman. If you recall the story, the woman asked Jesus four questions, permitting him to answer and to witness. The first question she asked was prompted by an unusual attitude on the part of Jesus. He, although a Jew, treated this Samaritan woman with respect. Never before had a Jew so treated her and she was amazed. "How come . . .?" she asked. And the opportunity was there.

Jesus had done a questionable act.

Could it be that the reason our opportunities to give a natural and convincing witness are so few is because the questions our lives raise are so few.

What should there be about the Christian that raises questions? Is it not to be expected that there should be a quality of life about a Christian that causes others to wonder? A steadiness, a patience, a vibrancy, an inner glow, a faith in the hour of tragedy, a peace in the time of fear.

Should there not be a quality in a Christian's relationship with others that raises questions? The attitude towards the disagreeable neighbor, the lonely girl in the office, or the social outcast. Should there not be a "second mile" quality and "the other cheek" attitude that has no natural explanation and that causes people to ask "Why do you . . .?"

What about your home and family life and the attitude of husband and wife to each other? Is there anything sufficiently Christian to make this apparent to those with whom we associate, causing them to wonder why this home is different?

How about the life in the church? Is there an atmosphere when the church gathers which causes a visitor in the group to wonder what it is all about?

I would like to believe that the answer to these questions is, "yes." There should be a supernatural quality to the Christian life that causes the non-Christian to ask, "How come . . .?" This is more than moral living, more than legalism, more than a pleasing personality. This calls for that supernatural element in life that Paul referred to when he wrote "If any man be in Christ, he is a new creation."

Peter said, "Be ready at anytime to give a quiet and reverent answer to any man who wants a reason for the hope that you have within you."

Peter must have assumed that Christians would live a questionable life.

The Samaritan Heresy

Most of us are guilty of it. As did the Samaritan woman, we equate worship with a certain setting—Jerusalem or this mountain. We go even further. We identify worship with form—whether or not we "liked the service."

The story is well known of the two friends of widely differing religious backgrounds who accompanied each other to their respective churches. And the story relates how satisfying each found the service to which he was accustomed and how meaningless he found the service in his friend's church.

The usual moral of the story is that the experience of worship is dependent upon a setting and a form that is familiar and to which we are conditioned. There is no doubt much to be said for a setting and a form in which the worshipper feels at home. But this very familiarity may be as great a threat to worship as a new setting or a strange form. The comfort we experience with a form made sacred by years of observance and hallowed memories may be confused with a vital and transforming experience of worship.

Another peril is our confusing of an aesthetic and emotional experience with worship. The beauty of the sanctuary, the quality of the music, the emotional tide of the service, or the stimulation of the sermon results in a satisfying experience too easily confused with true worship.

Beauty is surely to be preferred to ugliness, and order to chaos. But we must realize that the form is not the substance. We need to be aware of the danger of the form and setting becoming the end rather than the means to the end—the end being true worship.

Jesus called for an experience that transcends place and form. True worship is in spirit and in reality. This happens when we meet God who has promised to be already present when and where two or three meet. It happens when his holiness confronts our sinfulness; when his strength, our weakness; when we hear his word and he hears our cry; when we are awed both by his holiness and his great love; when in wonder and obedience we cry, "My Lord and My God."

There is also the horizontal element in worship. The Bible speaks of the two or the three being gathered. It speaks as well of the need to be reconciled to the brother before the gift is presented upon the altar. To paraphrase the words of the Apostle John, "How can we say we have worshipped God when there is something between us and our brother?"

The prophets would remind us that obedience is far better than ritual—elaborate or simple. Christ would remind us that honesty and sincerity are far more important than setting or place.

The Double Threat

We are preoccupied with violence. The legitimacy of violence and the necessity for its use are proclaimed by influential leaders of the academic and black communities and sanctioned by some ecclesiastical spokesmen.

Those not advocating violence are preoccupied with its threat. They see a deterioration in law and order that threatens the very foundation of an organized society. Life and property of law-abiding citizens are in peril. If violence is unchecked, our universities and colleges will become hideouts for modern day Robin Hoods and our cities pockets of armed rebellion.

The counter danger to this condition of violence and protest is the strong arm of a strong man. The majority of society frightened and desperate turns to one who promises peace on street and campus. All he asks is the waiving of the rights of the individual for the good of the whole. His platform will be law and order. His rallying cry will be God and country.

Conservative Christians are rightly concerned about respect for law and they themselves are law respecting citizens. This respect for law and their theological position makes them peculiarly responsive to this authoritarian approach. If I evaluate correctly what I read in the conservative Christian press, it has stood with the military against its attackers, with the police rather than the courts, and with capital rather than labor. I recently heard an evangelical leader say, "I see a fascist horseman on the horizon, and the evangelicals are piping him in."

What can a Christian do in light of these two threats to our existence as a free society? Let me offer several suggestions which are neither exhaustive nor profound.

We should recognize the legitimacy of much of the protest that is taking place. We will surely deplore the methods of violence. We may even question the value of non-violent means of protest and choose not to support them. But we cannot deny the justification for a voice to be raised against conditions in our society.

We need to inform ourselves as Christians as to the real issues and conditions behind the protest. We will find that there are professional agitators and outside financial support. But if this is the extent of our information, we are ill-informed. The impersonal quality of a large university, the hopelessness of the black community; the inner conflict in a young man's mind who is asked to participate and indeed give his life in a war that is questioned militarily, diplomatically, and morally, are very real issues and will not go away if protest is silenced.

As Christians we must clearly deplore violence but just as clearly identify ourselves with the legitimate issues. To support violence is obviously sub-Christian if not anti-Christian. To refuse to identify with the legitimate issues is to admit that we have no better solution. A former president of the United States has said that those who resist peaceful change make violent revolution inevitable.

Let us be wary of the leader who offers easy and quick solutions to difficult and deeply rooted problems. Let us be doubly wary of one who promises to deal with the unrest and the protest without a serious and costly attack upon the causes.

The Christian is a minister of reconciliation bearing the message of reconciliation. It is the Christian's opportunity—and a unique one—to bring upon any situation the resources of the Gospel which changes men, atmosphere, and conditions.

Nor should we forget that we are "protest-ants" and that our forefathers were guilty of protesting. There is the danger that should a strong government arise that resorts to strong armed methods—limiting freedom of speech and assembly and equating dissent with treason—we may well discover that we have more in common with the protestors than we know and that we have bound our arms to keep our hands from shaking.

Fatigue or Obesity

I recently heard of some members of a congregation who were dissatisfied because, in their words, "we are not getting fed." What all may have been involved in that statement I do not know. Obviously there was in their minds either a deficiency or an insufficiency in the spiritual diet.

This remark called to mind an experience of some years ago. I had an opportunity to share briefly in a church's program. As I listened to the laymen of that church recount their program I was fatigued. The emphasis was upon action and program to the neglect of biblical study and preaching. I concluded that here was a church overworked and underfed.

In contrast to this experience was another association I had had. This group had long sat under strong expository preaching. This diet of biblical preaching was not accompanied by an equal emphasis upon action. Here was a congregation carrying well worn Bibles which they knew very well. They spent their time discussing doctrines and dispensations and those who did not agree with them. Their principal spiritual activity was attending Bible conferences and camp meetings. My impression of this congregation was that it was overfed and underworked.

Healthy spiritual life calls for the strong meat of the word and the strenuous exercise of obedience. Nourishment comes from hearing the word. Exercise comes from doing it.

Jesus was aware of the spiritual peril that finds satisfaction in hearing and knowing the word but not doing it. He concluded his great sermon by the command: "Be ye doers of the word and not hearers only."

He likewise knew the need for nourishment in the Christian life when he gave Peter the thrice repeated commission "Feed my sheep."

If we expect the members to work, they need to be fed well. And if they are well fed they had better be worked hard.

Failure to keep the proper balance will result in either spiritual fatigue or spiritual obesity. Either condition could lead to spiritual death.

The Joy of Cooking
On a Wood Stove

Quite likely I already have lost half of my audience. My feminine readers may well ask, "What does he know about cooking on a wood-fired stove?" I know a little. I carried many an armload of wood to fire my mother's stove. I dipped hot water from the reservoir and I warmed myself at the open oven. But when it comes to cooking my answer would have to be, "I know very little."

But let me tell you a story.

It was only a few years ago that a missionary related an experience she had while on deputation. She and her husband were in Kansas being entertained in a Kansas home of more than average means. In the course of the visit she joined the wife of the home in her kitchen. There she found her cooking on a wood-fired stove.

The hostess was somewhat self-conscious of this out-dated kitchen appliance. So she explained: "We intended to purchase a new stove this year and had laid some money aside for it. But just about the time we were ready to buy one, an urgent call for funds came for missions. So we sent our money there instead and decided the old stove would do another year."

Sometime after hearing this story I related the incident to a Sunday morning audience and then asked the question: "Do you know the joy that comes from cooking on a wood stove?" And I noticed in the audience a lady who responded to that question with a radiant expression. And then I recalled that in this home, above average in means and culture, and noted for generous giving to the program of the church, there was still a wood-fired cook stove.

Now should anyone think that this is a joy reserved for the fairer sex let me tell you about a car and the joy that results from driving an old one.

I was in California and it was there I saw the car. I saw it first hand. I rode in it. It had seen better days and it was one of the economy makes to begin with. In the back seat there was a supply of used clothing. The glove compartment contained medical supplies. The owners of the car were giving their service among the migrant laborers of central California. And I venture that they knew a joy in driving this old car that few car owners know anything about.

Perhaps it was the contrast between this car and another one that I had seen only a few months previously that has caused it to be so imprinted upon my memory.

The other car was big and new and shiny. It was a late model of an expensive make. The owner was a pious Christian. He was also a witnessing one. Religious stickers adorned the bumper. But I seriously question if this unknown owner knew anything of the joy experienced by the owners of the California car.

Now I am not against progress and comfort. I hope that none of my feminine readers needs to cook on a wood-fired stove (although I know some do). I trust that my readers all own cars that take them there and back without undue question and expense. But it is still true that there is a joy that comes in doing without for the sake of Christ and his work that is not found in first looking after ourselves.

There is a Christian style of life that is distinct from the non-Christian. It is more than ethical and moral conduct. It is more than observing the rituals of the church, whether high church or low. One of the characteristics of this life is joy. It is a joy found in what we have received by grace and through the indwelling Spirit. It is also a result of an attitude towards life and how we live it. There is a joy in giving rather than keeping. There is a joy in losing that is never found in saving.

This style of life is determined by the degree of our Christian compassion and the world's need. What evidence is there in our style of life that we really care?

Could it be that the widow's rule of stewardship has something to say? Put simply it is this: Christian stewardship is not measured by how much we give but by how much we keep. We are easily impressed with the amount given. Jesus was impressed by how much was left. He immortalized the unknown widow because she gave out of her poverty, her very necessity—"All the living that she had."

I wonder so much why the widow was so liberal in her giving. And of all who gave their gifts that day I wonder who experienced the greatest joy.

The Recovery of Discipline

In recent editorials we have expressed our conviction that the temper of the times calls for a renewed emphasis upon the quality of discipleship. If the church is to be salt and light, there needs to be a recovery of disciplined Christian living.

This quality of discipleship will be marked by an experience that is Christ-centered and Spirit-born. It must move a man at the very center of his being. It deals with loyalties and values. The test of its validity will be the new man in Christ. One of the evidences of this new life will be obedience to the biblical pattern for this new life, especially that which Jesus taught.

In neither experience nor in obedience does a man act alone. The new birth is a birth into a family—the church. The unity of which Jesus spoke in the Gospel of John, the use of the word *Brethren* throughout the New Testament, and Paul's use of the body as a symbol of the Christian community all point to the truth that no one is a Christian "in his own way."

If this interpretation of the role of the church in the life of a Christian is correct, then the church has a responsibility to each member. This responsibility includes helping to determine what discipleship means and assisting the members to fulfill the call to obey. It is to this role of the church that we want to turn our attention.

The church has taken varied approaches to how it aids the members in living out their faith.

There is the tendency on the part of some to relegate obedience to the direction of the Spirit. If a man is truly converted and if he takes advantage of the means of grace—scriptures and sacraments— the Spirit will lead him into a life of obedience and discipleship. But neither the Great Commission nor the Epistles give support to the idea that if the heart is right everything will come out all right. The need for teaching is explicit in the New Testament.

There is another position taken in which the church deals in biblical principles but not specifics unless the Bible is clearly specific. Temperance, stewardship, separation, love, and forgiveness are principles which should guide the Christian's life. The expressions of these principles become largely a personal matter. It is obvious that the Bible presents great principles which should guide a Christian in his style of life. But it becomes so easy to give assent to principles but to not see the application of these principles, especially in one's own life.

This leads to a third position in which the church not only identifies the principles proclaimed in the Bible but seeks to apply these principles in concrete forms. Most of us are too blinded by prejudice and selfishness to transform principles into practice without the help and counsel of the church and our fellow Christians. This is especially true in our interpersonal relationships and social involvements.

A fourth position finds the church not only serving in the role of teacher and counsellor, but also in the requiring of obedience. Obedience is taken seriously and discipline is exercised to assure the integrity of the church and the redemption of the brother. The term legalism has been associated with this position.

As good as are the intentions of this approach, it has some serious shortcomings.

It gives a false sense of security. The logical outcome is to assume that obedience to laws is identical to a saving relationship with Christ.

It is an impossible approach. There is no limit to the details to be spelled out. The multitude of Sabbath laws in Jesus' time reveals the logical end of legalism.

It is selective. Some biblical principles can be codified into rules; others cannot. And it is the weightier matters, to use a phrase coined by Jesus, that resist being codified.

Finally, it cuts the very nerve of Christian discipleship which is based on love and relationship. Laws may force a husband to support his wife and children but no law has been passed that can force him to love them.

In fact, legalism is too easy a way to express Christian discipleship. For Christian discipleship is neither assent to truth nor observance of law. It is a commitment of life—a relationship of trust—a denial and death of self.

What then can the church do?

Basic must be the conviction that repentance and faith imply obedience. Obedience is not an option; it is the essence of discipleship. This needs to be crystal clear in the evangelistic and nurture ministries of the church.

Membership in the church is a serious act which carries obligations as well as benefits. Membership assumes that the one seeking membership has been born of the Spirit and is willing to assume the responsibilities and obligations of identification and fellowship with a group of believers. He is sensitive to the will of the group. He measures his life by the counsel of the church.

The church is not only concerned that the members know what their attitudes and practice should be, but also that they observe to do them. What is the alternative to a legalism? What about discipline?

It is here that the fellowship of the Christian community has its real test and its finest hour. Having made the fellowship meaningful by an understanding of conversion and membership, it is then by love and concern, prayer and study, sharing and counsel that the life of the group is maintained.

We should understand that discipline is not primarily punitive but redemptive. The purity of the church is its secondary concern. Its primary concern is the redemption of the brother and the sensitivity of us all to the life of obedience.

The Dandelion Principle

With the coming of spring, along with the robins and the tulips come the dandelions. Each spring I have a bumper crop. In fact usually one of the best in our area. Mine are large and they are plentiful.

I am especially conscious of my stand of dandelion because my next door neighbor has so few. The lush green of his lawn and the golden haze on mine leave no doubt as to the location of the property line. My only consolation is that his lawn is to the west of mine and the prevailing westerlies blow the seeds east.

Now I know that in spite of their brilliant color dandelions are not highly regarded. No respectable homeowner puts up with a yellow haze on his lawn in the spring. So I have made a study of dandelion control and have gathered some knowledge, considerable experience, and limited success.

A natural reaction is to cut off the yellow flowers and thus keep the seed from maturing and spreading. This I do, but I find it rather futile. They continue to produce flowers. The plants refuse to die and the roots send out rhizomes to start new plants.

I have attacked them by hoe and sharp knife. This I have found more effective but far more taxing. To cut them below the crown is better than only cutting off the flowers but it is much like plucking the tares from the wheat. It takes care of the dandelion but takes care of some grass as well. The size of my lawn wearies my spirit, to say nothing of my back.

Then I discovered chemicals. I have learned that to spray the plants with weed killer will result in their turning black and dying. There are chemicals that I can spread across my lawn which take care of dandelions and other weeds with much less labor but more expense.

Now, I found a rather interesting fact in my research. In addition to all these methods of elimination I was advised to fertilize the lawn. Get the grass to grow and the dandelions will be much less of a problem. I found some confirmation of this theory in that where my grass was the most sparse there the dandelions were the more plentiful and where the lawn was thick the dandelions were fewer.

And as I cut and dug and sprayed I recalled the words of the Master:

"When the unclean spirit is gone out of a man, he walketh through dry places, seeking rest; and finding none, he saith, I will return unto my house whence I came out. And when he cometh, he findeth it swept and garnished. Then goeth he, and taketh to him seven other spirits more wicked than himself; and they enter in, and dwell there: and the last state of that man is worse than the first" (Luke 11:24-26).

Just as in nature, so in the realm of the spirit a vacuum is an unstable and perilous condition. An empty life, just as a poor lawn, is in peril. Lives that are filled with the positive and noble graces, minds occupied with meaningful and great ideas, lives devoted to gracious and unselfish deeds are more secure from the destructive attitudes and actions that seek to invade our lives.

The dandelion principle has meaning for the life of a congregation. God help that congregation where the concept of the Christian faith and Christian life is to dig out the dandelions. Where the emphasis is upon the exposure and expurgating of evil. Where the concept of discipleship is based upon what a Christian does not do rather than on what he does.

Let the pastor of the congregation feed the members out of the resources of the Word; let him expose sin but with even greater zeal proclaim the resources of grace. Let him lead his people in a life of loving devotion and Christ-like ministry. If he does this, God will honor his Word and the life of the congregation will be productive of the fruit and gifts of the Spirit. Spiritual dandelions will be hard pressed to grow.

What is true in the life of a congregation is equally true in each of our lives. It is so easy for us to put the emphasis in our Christian lives upon what we do not do. We have "put off . . . the former conversation" but have not "put on the new man." We emphasize "be not conformed to this world" but the "renewing of your mind" does not come through quite so clearly.

And so our lives are "swept and garnished" but empty—a vacuum inviting the entry of attitudes and thoughts even more demonic than those put off. Their number is legion—bitterness, evil speaking, jealously, resentfulness, criticism. Paul knew the peril of the emptiness of the spirit when he wrote:

"Whatsoever things are true, honest, just, pure, lovely, think on these things."

One of the tragic yet in some respects hopeful evidences of our emptiness is its effect upon the youth. I would venture that an honest response from our youth as to what they understand we mean by living the Christian life would be largely a negative concept—cutting, digging, and spraying dandelions. I dare say that even their understanding of faith has negative overtones.

We have bequeathed to our children a legacy of emptiness. Their lives are "swept and garnished" and empty. The culture of our day which has such an appeal to our youth is in many respects the demon returning with his seven cohorts to occupy this spiritual vacuum.

The hopeful sign is the recognition by a new generation of the hollowness of their lives and ours and the constructive ways they seek and efforts they make to fill this spiritual void.

For some of us our only plea in the hour of that great judgment will be based on the things we have not done. Is it not about time we feed the lawn and spend less time digging dandelions?

"I Believe in the Holy Spirit"

The ancient creeds of the church did not give much space to the doctrine of the Holy Spirit. Historically they were formulated at the time the doctrine of the person and work of Christ was being hammered out. Therefore a major portion of each of the historic creeds was devoted to Christology. Somewhere in his writings E. Stanley Jones points out the unhappy state of Christendom at the time the creeds were being formulated, when the church could say no more about the Holy Spirit than "I believe in the Holy Spirit."

Perhaps Dr. Jones was correct. Surely something had occurred in the life of the church during those first centuries that had replaced the role which the Spirit had filled in the early days of the church. On the other hand the centrality of Christ in the life of the church must be maintained. Nor is it the amount of space given in the creeds that is crucial but rather the depth of meaning one gives to the short but profound statement "I believe in the Holy Spirit."

An Historical Event

To affirm one's belief in the Holy Spirit confronts one with Pentecost. The church and its members must come to terms with the significance of that event. The biblical position is that with Pentecost a new age came. The time foretold by the prophets and promised by Christ was now here. Divine resources were now available in a manner not heretofore possible.

We fail to understand the New Testament message if we believe we can practice the gospel ethics of love and compassion and enjoy the experiences referred to in the epistles without coming to terms with the events of the early chapters of the Acts.

Something new had happened. Ordinary men and women were transformed into a joyous, loving, fearless community of faith. I do not believe that this transformation can be adequately explained without recognizing that their lives had been invaded from beyond themselves. The Holy Spirit had taken possession. The supernatural now characterized their lives and ministry.

A Community Experience

The affirmation concerning the Holy Spirit in the creed is immediately followed by two statements concerning the community of faith. "I believe in the Holy Spirit, the holy Christian Church, the Communion of Saints . . ." I do not have a high theory of inspiration as it relates to creedal statements, but I find it most interesting—and I believe significant—that the statements on the Holy Spirit and on the church are tied so closely together. In this affinity the creed reflects the New Testament pattern.

The immediate result of Pentecost was the creation of community. Read Acts 2:41-47. Notice the description of those who experienced Pentecost. ". . . they continued in the apostles' . . . fellowship, and in breaking of bread . . . all that believed were together, and had all things common . . . one accord . . . breaking bread from house to house."

Whatever else one could say about the Pentecostal experience, it is evident that there was created a new relationship among those who experienced it. One could venture the assertion that one of the tests of the validity of the Spirit's visitation is whether or not oneness and fellowship are fostered.

Equally significant to the creation of community is the manner in which the Spirit honored and worked through this community of faith. Few are the accounts in the Acts where it is recorded that the Holy Spirit comes upon *one* individual in isolation. The account of the Apostle Paul with Ananias is such a one.

But over against this we recall that not just select individuals, but all of the 120 were filled on the Day of Pentecost (Acts 2). Upon the release of the Apostles in Acts 4 it is recorded that "they were *all* filled with the Holy Spirit . . ." (v. 31). The Samaritan mission of Philip was climaxed when upon the arrival of the Apostles ". . . they (the new believers) received the Holy Ghost" (Acts 8). In the house of Cornelius as Peter was preaching it is recorded that "the Holy Ghost fell on *all* them which heard the Word" (Acts 10:44). Then there is the interesting incident at Ephesus when Paul laid his hands upon about twelve disciples of John the Baptist and it is recorded that "the Holy Spirit came on *them*" (Acts 19).

In contrast with these New Testament accounts is the strong

tendency in our day to individualize the Holy Spirit's visitation and separate it from the community. We envision each person seeking for the experience of the fullness of the Spirit and finding his need met outside the context of the wider seeking fellowship. It seems so right. Each of us must come to terms with God's demands for his own individual life. But I question if our position can stand the test of the New Testament. There is a corporate seeking that brings individual and corporate fullness.

This tension between the individual and the group is clearly maintained in the Pentecost account: the "cloven tongues . . . sat upon *each* of them. And they were *all* filled . . ." The spiritual awakenings that have been reported on college campuses and within congregations have had this similar biblical tension. There is more to it than individuals being moved and filled by the Spirit. Communities (academic and congregational) are being moved corporately in a strange and sovereign way by the Spirit of God.

I believe there is a hunger in the land. I believe there is a hunger within the church. Let us open ourselves as a church—as a community of faith—to the sovereign movings of the Holy Spirit. Pray that in true Pentecost fashion it may not only fall on *each* but that *all* may be filled.

So when we say that we believe in the Holy Spirit, let us be orthodox and biblical and include with this affirmation our belief in the holy Christian Church and the Communion of Saints.

The Graduate

Dear Graduate,

If I understand what I read and hear, there is seemingly a gulf between the world in which you have lived for the past four years and my world. I represent the establishment—parents, church, business, and government. You have been critical of us. We have permitted injustice and poverty to exist. We have trusted in arms and warfare. You accused us of being more concerned with property than with people. We judged life by the Dow-Jones averages and the G.N.P. And one could go on!

You are near enough right to make it hurt. Perhaps that is why we are so defensive. At least that is one of the reasons. There are others. We—that is my generation—have done a few things; we are not a total loss. We see much more to be done but find it takes time. We are willing to work through the structures of our society and church. Indeed we feel we must or chaos will be our lot. Evolution which used to have a bad connotation is now a good word. We prefer it to revolution.

And I suppose we are a bit defensive because it looks so much easier to you than it does to us. We pride ourselves in being realists. We know the facts of life and the nature of man, and our youthful idealism has been refined.

It would be easy to disregard this gulf by assuming that a few years of experience will bridge it—a family to feed, a mortgage to pay, an employer to satisfy, a community or church project which we supported, tabled. Then you too will see our side of all of this.

I am not going to take the easy way. Indeed I hope you do not succumb to the pressures of your new world. We need those qualities which we have seen evidenced during these years you have been a student. We need them badly.

We need the idealism. The faith and hope that things can be changed. We have prided ourselves in being realists. Probably we are more cynical than realistic. We need an infusion into our communities and churches of those who do not know it cannot be done. Unaware that it is impossible, you do it.

We would caution you, in your idealism, to be aware of the cosmic mutation that has affected individuals and society. The self-centeredness of man and the desire for power must be faced. This will temper your idealism, but do not let it destroy it. Indeed it may save you from becoming cynical.

Bring with you your commitment. We have not always agreed with your causes and your methods, but we are impressed with your commitment. You care. How different from days past when the mark of the educated man was to remain an objective observer—uncommitted—like a Greek god unmoved by the human situation.

We need people who care. Men who are moved with compassion. Men who will stake their honor and their fortunes for a cause they feel deeply about.

Bring with you your desire for reality and your hatred of the phony. There is an increasing number of us who are tired of substituting form for reality and words for deeds. We need you in our local congregations. Most of us spend most of our time just keeping the wheels turning. Hopefully the Spirit of God can speak through you to us and new meaning and reality can come to the local church.

We need you in the larger area of the church. Some of you have said "Christianity, No! Jesus, Yes!" I think I sense what you mean. The church has been a body without a head—a grotesque thought. On the other hand a head without a body is equally grotesque. If you mean that the church must become the Church—responsive to Christ and experiencing his power and life and love—then I say we need you desperately.

So, welcome graduate. Do not cop out nor sell out. It may not be an easy experience for either of us. It should be a great one, however.

Literary Societies
and Wineskins

In my college days I was a member of the Goethean Literary Society. There were two societies on the Franklin and Marshall campus. Both had a long and distinguished history. They each owned their own building on the campus. These buildings were built by the alumni of their respective societies.

I was a member in the waning days of literary societies. Our Friday evening attendance was not large but the debates were heated, if not relevant, and the papers presented had some of the marks of erudition. To be elected president of one of the societies was a prestigious honor.

Those were the good old days!

But they were fast coming to a close. I question if there are many literary societies meeting on college campuses anymore. There must have been a reason for their existence and the role they had in college life. There is likewise a reason for their passing from the scene. I do not intend to analyze the reason for either their existence or demise. I only use this to illustrate that institutions and forms come and go. And somehow the literary society is no longer the form for learning and experience that was once real and meaningful. Obviously, the learning experience has continued to go on in new forms and through new institutions. Not one of us will be too upset by the passing of the literary society, but the principle expressed in its passing is valid in every area of life. When forms and patterns no longer are viable and meaningful means of experience, they will eventually cease. They may be prolonged by any number of methods and for high purposes, but their end is sure.

This is also true within the church.

I probably did not need to spend this long a preface to get to my point. We are all aware that forms and patterns and programs within the church are in ferment. Indeed, the institutional church is suspect to an increasing number of youth and even adults. They feel that the forms and even the institution are not a channel but a curtain, not an aid but a hindrance to spiritual reality and the grace of God.

We will be better prepared for these changing times if we keep a number of truths in perspective.

First: Form is not identical to reality. Form is necessary but it is not the essence. Jesus spoke of wine and wineskins. The purpose of wineskins is to hold the wine. If they fail to do this they are no longer of value—indeed they are a liability. The wine is the essence. It is for the preservation and the transmitting of the wine that the wineskin exists. There comes a time, if I understand Jesus correctly, when the old wineskins need to give way to new. New forms are needed to transmit reality.

I dare say that this is a principle we find difficult to learn in the church. Too often we identify form with reality. Practices and programs become sacred by long observance. And we assume that having at one time been the bearers of reality, they must still be such. We do not distinguish between the form itself and the reality it is intended to convey.

Now this means that those forms which seem so important to us—worship at eleven o'clock Sunday morning—a pulpit at the front of the sanctuary—the sanctuary itself—the graded Sunday school—the midweek service—the quarterly communion—the men's fellowship—are only forms, and are legitimate forms only when they are means of communicating God's grace to human need. But they are not the essence.

A second truth we need to remember is that forms and institutions exist for people, not people for them. Nothing was more sacred to the Jews of Jesus' time than the Sabbath. This holy institution had a long tradition. Rooted in the creation itself, it was formalized by law and supported by the prophets and a multitude of traditions so that men were in virtual bondage to the Sabbath. But Jesus dealt institutionalism a devastating blow when he said that the Sabbath was created for man and not man for the Sabbath.

Stated simply this means that people are more important than forms and institutions. So instead of bemoaning the lack of support for existing programs, we would do better if we would ask ourselves the question: Do the old forms still carry reality and meaning, or are new forms needed to meet the need of the people whom the institution is meant to serve?

Dedicated people can continue to maintain programs and forms indefinitely even after they have ceased to meet men's needs. But sensitive people will be disturbed and will seek new forms to serve the new age. I do not have space to point out the vast changes which have taken place in our society in the last fifty years—communication—transportation—urbanization—education—economics—mobility. Have we taken these changes into account or are we still patching up forms and patterns and concepts which were formalized in the late nineteenth century and the early decades of the present one?

Third: It is not easy to be constructive in our approach to traditional patterns of form and expression. Our approach is either to conserve the past or to discard it. It is much easier to defend or attack than it is develop new and viable forms.

There is, of course, something to be said for both conserving and attacking the present patterns. An old wineskin may be better than no wineskin at all. Forms are essential to give expression to reality and it may well be that the old is better than no form at all. So it is understandable that when forms and institutions are threatened and chaos seems to be the order of things, concerned people will rise in defense of the security they have known and seek to conserve it.

It is likewise understandable that those who sense the inadequacies of the present patterns are critical of them. It is certainly easier to see the sickness of a situation than it is to prescribe a cure. Nor should we necessarily demand that those who detect the inadequacies of present patterns remain silent unless they can offer alternatives.

These alternatives will arise out of the tension which results from those who would conserve and those who would discard. Alternatives will result from conversation between those who are concerned with order and form and those who cry for meaning and reality.

History is on the side of change. Societies and institutions unwilling to meet the demand for change are buried under the sands of time or exist in archives and history books. We need to do more than patch the old wineskins or postpone the inevitable by novel plans and sensational publicity. Nor is change for the sake of change the answer. The future belongs to those who open themselves to the reality of God and use those forms and means which are natural and effective in communicating this reality to a needy world.

Not By Bread Alone

A number of years ago a furniture store near where we lived furnished "a house" (they called it "The Penthouse") which was then opened to the public. A friend visited this house and related her observations. She was impressed by the very fine furnishings of all the rooms with the exception of the kitchen—this otherwise well appointed house had a very ordinary kitchen.

I did not see this house but I had some reactions to this friend's observations. Since, as far as I know, this furniture dealer did not sell custom-built kitchens, it was quite likely that this area of the house suffered in comparison. However, my intuitive reaction was that perhaps the kitchen was not as ordinary as the friend observed. I wondered if she had judged it in light of her own experience. Although the furnishings in the other rooms were outstanding as compared to similar rooms in her home, the kitchen came out second best. For among us the kitchen is a very important room and is equipped accordingly.

And well it may. Here a mother and wife spends a great portion of her working hours. Meal time for a family should be a high occasion. For many this is the only time when all members are together—and even this takes some doing. The health and well-being of the family depends upon proper nourishment and the financial well-being of most homes is closely related to what happens in the kitchen.

The kitchen is an area of our homes that has been rather adequately provided for. But how many of our homes have a library—a place set aside and equipped for the nurture of the mind and the spirit? It may bear another name, but is there a place of solitude and retreat where one can be alone and where there are resources to build the spirit and the mind?

Now, I know that this is somewhat unrealistic in view of the high cost of building but it is not unrealistic to predict a poverty of spirit if our kitchens are well equipped but no provision made for feeding the mind—for man does not live by bread alone.

Our homes are becoming smaller and we live in closer and closer proximity to each other. The radio and record player and television compete to be heard. For young and old, and for individual and family health, there is the need for a sanctuary—a place to think, to read and to pray. I propose no easy solution. I only state an urgent need.

A second concern is to provide within the context of the home the atmosphere and facility that will nurture the mind and spirit. Our generation has a problem unknown to those preceding. Into

our homes has come television. Its purpose is primarily entertainment. It can be a great thief of time. It is also a creator of values
and ideals—many of which are contrary to those to which we hold.

How does one counter these values and the influence of this
medium on our lives? There is of course the "off" switch, and we
need to know where it is and how to use it. This is only part of the
answer. For even if effective it would result in a vacuum—a perilous and unstable situation. To counter the influence of other
media there is that of the printed page. Here is an opportunity to
shape the form of the values and ideals to which we wish the family
to be exposed. Fill the shelves with books and cover the table with
magazines which inform, inspire, and build!

The discipline of reading needs to be discovered or recovered.
Parents by example and direction need to establish this discipline
in the lives of their children. The lack of reading is to the mind
what the refusal of eating is to the body. Through literature the
wisdom of the sages and the ages has been preserved and transmitted. Our acquaintance with great minds and exposure to great
ideas comes through the printed page. The knowledge of the
world in which we live and the history of civilizations past is
available to him who reads. One's ability to judge the emotional
appeals of the extremists—right or left—will be largely determined by one's own knowledge developed through reading.

The child who brings home from the community or church
library an arm full of books already has factors working for his
well-being. They may be Dr. Seuss books or stories of imaginative
sports heroes, but here is a child who is learning the pleasure of
reading—one of life's greatest pleasures—and a discipline which
will bring knowledge not otherwise available. To learn the
enjoyment of reading is one of the better ways to keep the TV in its
proper role.

A public library is a credit to any community and a church
library to any congregation, but we also need books of our own.
There should be books available within our reach and surrounding us with their silent influence. Magazines for the age and
interest groups of the family, Christian books and magazines
which convey Christian truth and values with integrity and
relevance.

Books and magazines take money. But it becomes really a matter
of value. We usually find money to do what needs to be done. If we
do not believe that it is necessary to have good magazines lying
around the house, if we do not feel that it is essential to expose our
minds to quality books, if we think that our children will receive a
balanced mental and spiritual diet on twenty hours a week of

television and two to three hours of Christian instruction, then we can save our money. Save it to keep the TV in repair, to buy gas and tires, and to purchase tranquilizers. It is a matter of values.

This is not an effort to idolize the "book-worm" or the social misfit who escapes to the world of books. This is an appeal to prepare ourselves and our children to live in a world where ideas and values are in mortal conflict. We believe that reading is our best way to understand man and his world and to evaluate ideas and philosophies, to distinguish between truth and error, and to judge the emotional presentations from other media.

One of the characteristics of our age, and even more so of the days ahead, is the absence of those traditional influences which aid in maintaining a Christian style of life. The popular media of our time—radio, television, movies—present a barrage of values in direct opposition to those held by the Christian. There remains one medium which offers a choice and the means to balance the impact on our mind. This remaining medium is literature.

What father among you who if his son asks for bread would give him a stone or if he asks for a book would give him bread?

Let's Talk about Money

We have a rather general agreement on principles. It is in their application that differences arise. We believe in "liberty and justice for all" but as a people we are divided right down the middle on the application. We consider modesty a Christian virtue but its application is another matter. The principle of stewardship is commonly recognized as a biblical concept and a Christian truth, but convert this principle to dollars and cents and one is accused of a superficial view of stewardship.

No matter if the principle is love, modesty, temperance, equality, justice, or stewardship, unless that principle becomes practical, it is of no earthly, or for that matter, heavenly good. If the road to hell is paved with good intentions, its road bed is built of lofty principles. Although mindful of the wider ramifications of stewardship, let's talk about money.

Let's talk about money because the Bible talks about it. In fact the Bible places a special significance on money. In certain cases prosperity was an evidence of God's approval. In other situations—

especially the prophets—wealth was suspect and God identified with those who did not have it. The New Testament warns against the desire for wealth and the love of riches. Jesus warned of their tendency to keep a man out of the kingdom. Paul made a rather broad and sweeping statement when he said that "The love of money is the root of all evil."

I am not suggesting that we should take vows of poverty. But I believe that the Bible points out that money relates in a unique way to our spiritual lives. Wealth or money has religious significance. It becomes the object of our faith and love. For it we give our lives. It brings power. It provides security. It purchases service. Its possession gives status and prestige. It gratifies pride. It replaces God. Paul writes "Beware of covetousnes, which is idolatry."

Now the point of all this is that when stewardship does not come to grips with money, it has failed to come to grips. So let's talk about money because Jesus talked about it and it is such a crucial part of our spiritual lives.

How Much?

Norman Wingert has written an interesting poem entitled "Countdown" in which he contrasts man's view of life and God's view.

> My days are numbered
> And God knows the sum;
> While I count up the years,
> He counts down.

As man "counts up" the years he has lived, God "counts down" the years he has left. It is so with stewardship. Man measures by what is given. God measures by what is left. This was the basis of Christ's commendation of the widow who gave her two mites while the rich threw great amounts into the treasury.

And most of us have considerable left—rather we keep a great deal for ourselves, for it takes so much for us to live. How many pairs of shoes can a man wear? How many coats does he have to have? It just could be that God is as concerned about the cost of a dress as he is its length, and the price of a suit as he is its color.

Parkinson's Second Law, which states that "expenditures rise to meet income," is as true about our personal and family incomes as it is with institutions and government. If we suddenly had our salaries doubled, most of us would find it just as difficult to pay our tithe. The demands on our money seem so necessary and reasonable. But the fact is that it takes so much for us to live—and the more we have, the more it takes. And church budgets suffer while ours soar.

Where to?

Responsible stewardship is not only concerned with the amount given or the amount retained, but also with the destination. Not all who say, "Lord, Lord," are doing his work. Some who do it, do it inefficiently—spending much of the dollar to raise a dollar resulting in a small percentage reaching the ultimate need.

Some build up assets over which they retain family control. A well known evangelical radio personality who was prominent several decades ago in the eastern states died leaving an estate reported to be in excess of a million dollars—much of which was left to his sons who are without Christian motivation. Much of this estate was the result of sincere Christians sending God's money in reponse to radio appeals. Incidents even more disturbing could be documented.

It is difficult to determine the true worth of a cause by the fervent and pious radio appeal or the attractive and persuasive brochures. Too many questions remain unanswered. We know too little about the style of life of those who are seeking our support—in fact, God's money. We know too little about the spirit and effectiveness of the work—is it cooperative or divisive. Nor do we know what portion of the dollar, for which we are stewards, arrives at the point of ultimate need.

Every so often one reads in the newspaper of the notorious "pigeon drop" in which a naive and trusting person (often an older person) turns over to a complete stranger a sizeable amount of cash in response to a convincing story and the promise of substantial gain. The results are predictable—both stranger and money disappear. We read and shake our heads at the credulity of some people. How could anyone be so naive. We would never give our money to a stranger! But are we as careful with God's money? In our investment of his funds are we as judicious as we are with our own?

Obviously we do not have the time nor the means to assure ourselves of the integrity of all the appeals which come to our attention. This points up the value of a brotherhood relationship. Here are programs—perhaps less glamorous but often more effective—over which through our own brethren we have control and knowledge. Those involved—administrator, teacher, nurse, evangelist—are known to the church and are from our own congregations and return to our churches. Their style and manner of life is known among us. These are not strangers. These are known to us.

Stewardship of God's resources calls for us to not only give sacrificially but to give wisely. As stewards we should give to those

causes which build rather than divide, which increase the kingdom of God rather than a man's estate, and which are characterized
by a sense of sacrifice consistent with the One whose name they
bear—he who came not to be ministered unto but to minister,
taking upon himself the form of a servant.

A Matter of Tenses

On some page in an old composition book there is a paragraph
or two on the use of "shall" and "will." I confess that I did not
master those paragraphs for I am not clear when I should use
"shall" or use "will." I do recall that the person of the subject
(first, second, or third) had a bearing as well as the intent of the
statement.

If it was the simple future that was meant this would call for a
certain combination of subject and verb. If an emphatic future was
intended then the combination would change. When a mother
says to her son "You will get a haircut tomorrow," is this a simple
future or a command?

Now, I have the impression that I am not the only one who is
confused. In fact the Christian church has problems. When Jesus
told his disciples "... Ye shall be witnesses unto me ..." was this a
statement of future fact or was this a command? Did Jesus mean
that his disciples *would* be witnesses or that they *should* be
witnesses?

Much that we hear and read assumes the latter interpretation.
People express a desire to do witnessing for Christ. Classes are held
and books written on how to witness. Numerous messages are
preached on calling people to witness—to neighbor, fellow
employee, customer, and others.

All this appears to me to be a crucial misunderstanding of Jesus'
statement. We have interpreted it as a command when it is really a
statement of fact. Witnessing is not something we should do, it is
something we are doing if we bear the name Christian. We may be
favorable witnesses or unfavorable ones, but witnesses we are—
there is no escape.

Let's attempt to recapture the primitive setting. Here were men
who had been with Jesus during his ministry. They were aware of

his death; they had seen him and talked with him following his resurrection. Now upon his ascension they would remain to carry out his commission to make disciples. Following the experience of Pentecost they, in the words of Peter and John, could not "but speak the things which we have seen and heard."

As Christ through the Holy Spirit and the proclamation of the gospel confronts men and women, Christians are his witnesses in this divine-human encounter. As he presses for a decision, we are part of the evidence. Are the claims of the gospel valid? Is the promise of new life authentic? To these crucial questions we are the witnesses—favorable or unfavorable.

Our confusion of witnessing as something we *should do* rather than something *we do* is compounded with a misunderstanding of the role. We are neither the prosecuting attorney nor the judge in the case. We are witnesses.

We are tempted to press the case, to seek for a decision, to question the subject. This is not the witnesses' role. It may be very proper to inquire of a person if he is a Christian, but this is not witnessing. It may be necessary to point out sin in a person's life, but again this is not witnessing. It may be essential to press for a decision, but this is not witnessing either.

The techniques of bringing men and women to a decision may be learned. The Scriptures which lead a person to see himself and to see the provisons of God's grace must be known and presented. It seems sometimes that we would much rather learn the techniques in order that we may fill the other roles rather than that of a witness. I suspect that one of the reasons—and perhaps the reason—is that these roles are much less demanding. The role of the prosecutor can be learned, the role of the judge is quite tempting, but the role of the witness must be experienced. The qualification of a witness is first-hand knowledge of the situation—"We cannot but speak of the things we have heard and seen." The blind man of John 9 may have lacked biblical and theological knowledge but when he said ". . . One thing I know, that, whereas I was blind, now I see," he was fulfilling the role of the witness in its pure and convincing form.

Now really what we need is not more classes in personal witnessing nor techniques. What we lack is not courage nor opportunity. Our real problem is an absence of a compelling experience with God that is evident in our life both in deed and word.

For too many of us the evidence of our lives is not very convincing. Let me ask if the peace and joy and love and compassion which are inherent in the Christian faith are obvious in our lives—obvious to our families, neighbors, fellow employees? Is there a commitment in our faith that is contagious? If there is, I suspect we will be asked to share it. But no matter if these virtues are present or absent, we are witnessing—for better or for worse. This is the missing ingredient in our evangelism—witnesses that provide convincing evidence rather than raise embarrassing questions. Witnesses who have not only a valid experience but a compelling one, the reality of which is contagious. Call it what you will—revival or renewal, we need a recovery of first-hand faith that is evident in a new life, a life with some of the supernatural in it.

The evangelist proclaims; the Holy Spirit convicts; Christians provide, in their personal and group relationships, a vital and convincing witness, "and the gates of hell shall not prevail against it."

Living in Tension

Tension is not generally considered good. The headaches and sleepless nights and shrill voice are not desirable. So by drugs and food, by activity and travel, and by faith and prayer we seek to relieve tension. [Most of us would approve the counsel a friend of mine would consistently offer at the appropriate time—"Stay loose."]

But tension in the world of ideas is both good and necessary. It is about this good meaning that I wish to reflect. To seek to escape the tension in ideas is to encourage intolerance and promote extremism. To seek to escape tension in the Christian faith is to deny or at least sell short a facet of Christian truth and to plant the seeds of heresy.

A foundational doctrine of the Christian faith is the Incarnation—"the Word became flesh and dwelt among us." The integrity of this doctrine depends upon keeping the humanity and deity of Christ in proper tension. The earliest Christian heresy (see I John 1) was the denial or the minimizing of Christ's humanity—he was not really man. Later heresies questioned his deity—he was not really God. Both sought to relieve the tension.

The writers of the creed recognized the need to maintain this tension when they stated that he was "very man of very man, and

very God of very God." There is the subtle drift for all us to relieve
this tension. We do it in violence to the biblical revelation and to
its great significance.

Or take the Christian doctrine of salvation, with its tension
between grace and works—God's role and man's. The gospel has
suffered at the hands of those who seek to resolve it by denying
man's role and seeing it entirely of God. The result is an absence of
good works and an abuse of God's grace—cheap grace that justifies sin rather than the sinner. We are aware as well of the tragic
consequence when the human role is emphasized at the expense of
grace, and reform replaces regeneration and pride replaces trust.

Even in the practical areas of the church's life it is necessary to
maintain a biblical tension.

Take evangelism and nurture. Some tension may well exist
because of an inadequate understanding of each. Some expect too
much from evangelism; others expect too little. Some count too
much on nurture; others see little need. But when both are seen in
their New Testament perspective, there still remains a tension
which must be maintained. Neither is sufficient or effective without the other. Indeed the two are clearly held in tension in the great
commission, "makes disciples . . . teaching . . ."

Then there are the horizontal and vertical relationships of the
Christian life—love for God and love for the neighbor. How easy it
is to give a priority to one of these in practice and give optional
status to the other. If it is love for God we stress, personal piety
becomes sentimentality as we neglect our obligation to our neighbor. But how dry becomes the wellspring of our concern for others
when this concern is not prompted by the living water of God's
Spirit.

The Christian church and denominations are divided because
they are unwilling to live in tension with these two commandments. We may learn a parable from the television screen, for only
when both the horizontal hold and the vertical hold are function-
ing properly do we have an acceptable picture.

Then there is the tension of freedom and discipline—the individual and the group. What is the attitude of the congregation
towards the member, and the responsibility of the member to the
fellowship? This tension is easily lost. There is the temptation to
delegate responsibility to the individual and the Spirit. Except for
the most dramatic of sins, the group exercises little responsibility
or discipline. Over against this position is the concern for the
image of the visible community and the desire to codify regulations and behavior and to insist upon conformity—even prior to
acceptance in the group.

The result of either practice is a high mortality rate. To recognize the need for growth and maturity by the newborn in Christ, and at the same time provide the discipline and concern of the family of faith, calls for the maintenance of tension. There is no escape.

The living with these tensions—and there are many more one could list—has various implications for the church and for each Christian.

First of all, we should not be disturbed by living in tension. It is biblical. It is a sign of health and maturity. Like the strings of a violin, tension is necessary. And just like the artist, we should not seek to eliminate tension but to keep it tuned to the true pitch as found in the Scriptures and supremely in Christ.

Second: One of God's means of maintaining the health of the church is through the granting of gifts. He gives some pastors and some prophets. He gives some teachers and some evangelists. A proper respect for gifts and a mature attitude towards tension will result in a respect for each gift rather than the honoring of some and the despising of others. One with a special gift sees himself as a worker together with those with other gifts, and not as a competitor.

Third: Let us be grateful for biblical tensions which may be a part of our own theology and church life. Beware of the easy answers! Whether it is the tension between crisis and nurture, holiness as an experience or a way of life, social concern and evangelism, respect for civil authority and obedience to God, or individual responsibility and the role of the fellowship, there will be a healthy tension if we are true to the Scriptures. And our ability as a church to communicate and minister will be enhanced as we maintain tensions and keep them constantly adjusted to the biblical norm.

Fourth: We dare not see these tensions as sapping our energy or destroying our initiative. The result of biblical tension is not the cancelling out of the two truths held in tension, but the discovery of new truth that is exciting and biblical. Out of the tension of grace and human effort rises the truth of obedience. The tension of love for God and love for neighbor produces the life of a love-motivated ministry. And from the tension of individual responsibility and a disciplined fellowship comes the new community of love and concern.

The Christian faith is like a fine-tuned instrument. The more closely it is tuned to the biblical revelation the truer will be the message. Its integrity and authenticity will depend upon its proper tension.

The Mystery of the Cross

Granted who Jesus was, the great miracle is not that he rose from the dead. Rather it is that he died on the cross. Surely for God to raise his Son does not seem incredible. But for God to let him die—to permit little men to abuse him and ridicule him, beat him and smite him, to scoff as he stumbled up Golgotha's hill and then to crucify him, and then to let him die—let him, who was the very image of God, the administrator of creation and one with the Father—die on a Roman cross. This is the real miracle and the divine mystery.

That God would work out his purpose by means of a cross was too much for the people in Paul's day. It was, he said, folly to the Greeks and a stumbling block to the Jews. What a way for God to work! What a way to come to man's aid! What a way to deal with sin and pride and hostility!

The people of Paul's day had their solutions to man's dilemma. For the Greeks it was wisdom. Man, by an understanding of himself and of his world, and through reason, logic, and philosophy, could unravel the meaning of life and find answers to man's dilemma.

For the Jews it was power. God would vindicate his people and his promise and bring in the promised kingdom by power. He would overthrow the oppressor. He would bring judgment on those who rejected his rule. The mark of his Anointed One would be his miracles. To be told that their Messiah had ended up on a Roman cross crucified by Roman soldiers was more than they could take. If it was foolishness to the Greeks it was a stumbling block to the Jews.

Paul says that in the cross the wisdom and the power of God have met. This was God's way to get to the heart of man's problem—sin. To understand and explain this mystery has been a challenge to the Christian mind since the disciples were scattered in the confusion of that Passover Friday. And just when we attempt to state its meaning in terms and figures we understand, the cross breaks out of our neat doctrinal statements. But in spite of our limitations to explain it, the church has found that response to it—to Jesus Christ crucified—has indeed been the wisdom and the power of God.

Surely one of the insights which the cross brings to us is that sin and evil were dealt with as God took unto himself this sin and evil and death. God was in Christ reconciling and forgiving. God had dealt with man's sin before—he sent fire from heaven and he sent water. He gave the law and a system of sacrifices. He sent nations to punish his people. He sent prophets to call them back.

But now it was different! The Word became flesh, the King a suffering servant. The kingdom symbol was to be a Roman cross. Here God, in the arena of man's existence, came to deal with man's need.

The parable commonly known as "The Prodigal Son," but better titled "The Waiting Father," has been described with justification as the most beautiful story in all literature. It quite aptly fulfills the purpose of its telling—to describe the joy of God at the return of a sinner. But when placed against the cross, it falls far short of describing the Father's love.

For the cross tells us that God did not wait at home looking down the road for the lost to return. Indeed, how could you and I ever have returned from the far country. We were guilty and knew only that the soul that sinneth, it shall die. More than guilty, we were enemies of God. We were in eternal flight to escape (Rom. 5:10). But more than that, as prodigals we were in bondage—sold unto sin. The memory of home, which haunts the hearts of all created in the image of God, could only be a taunting memory as man sat in prison guilty, bitter, and far from home.

But the Father did not wait. He left his home and began the search through the far country. He found his son—guilty, bitter, and in prison. And he offered pardon, himself accepting the punishment. He threw his arms around the prodigal. He paid the debt to free him.

This pilgrimage of the Father led him to a rugged hill outside Jerusalem. A hill called Calvary. And on this hill a cross was raised and on the sacred site redemptive history was enacted. Do not the traditional words of Christian faith describe man's plight and God's act.

"But God commendeth his love toward us, in that, while we were yet sinners, Christ died for us. Much more then, being now justified by his blood, we shall be saved from wrath through him. For if, when we were enemies, we were reconciled to God by the death of his Son, much more, being reconciled, we shall be saved by his life. And not only so, but we also joy in God through our Lord Jesus Christ, by whom we have now received the atonement" (Rom. 5:8-11).

The cross is still the *wisdom* of God. Man's need has not changed except to get more critical—guilty—estranged—enslaved. Neither law nor ritual, power nor prophets, learning nor culture have power to pardon, reconcile, and redeem.

To proclaim the message of the cross continues to demand the priority it did in Paul's day. But it must be proclaimed by more than word alone. The cross must become the pattern of the church who, as the body of Christ, continues to seek and to love; continues to forgive, reconcile, and redeem. The cross calls the church to leave the security and comfort of home to search the far country for the prodigal. To be where life is hard and hope is lost, and guilt and loneliness the common lot. And there to proclaim forgiveness and reconciliation and liberty—possible through the Cross of Christ.

"Four Days You Shall Labor"

The man across the luncheon table was speaking with the lady to his right. He was relating a recent conversation he had had with a young man. He had inquired of the youth as to his summer activity. The young man's reply was, "I am just praising the Lord."

Within the context of the conversation this appeared to mean that the young man was not gainfully or productively employed. He did not in the common parlance "have a job." He was free. He was using his freedom to "praise the Lord."

Both the man who reported the incident and the woman to whom he told it reacted with favor to the youth's response. The man stated that he felt rebuked by the young man's reply. The woman thought the response to be "just beautiful."

Now that may be a very narrow perspective from which to observe the current attitude towards work, but it is an indication of what has taken place in our society in respect to work.

Work has fallen upon hard times. It is more than a management-union problem. It is philosophical and theological. A generation has come of age which does not have the same regard for work which its parents and grandparents had.

In fact there has been a shift even among the parents. Leisure has for many replaced work as the purpose of life. Long and longer weekends, more holidays, assured vacations, and early retirement are the goal of those who work. The emphasis is upon the benefits for the worker rather than upon the contribution made by the work.

It would not be difficult to find reasons for this change in attitude towards work and find the evidence which would give a measure of justification for the change that has taken place.

Perhaps it was the "protestant work ethic," with its sense of stewardship and responsibility; perhaps it was the memory of the great depression with the bread lines; or perhaps it was just plain avarice which caused us to work hard to accumulate more and to glorify work and condemn idleness.

For many cleanliness and industry rivaled each other for that position next to godliness. If a man or a woman who was "easy-going" was converted, we assumed that it would change his or her style of life. He would now spend less time fishing and more time working around his property. A paint brush would replace the fishing pole in his hand and a needle and thread would replace the telephone in hers.

The result of all this was that with industry given such a high position in the list of Christian virtues, other aspects of life— culture, relationships, meditation, and education (except to improve one's ability to earn) were relegated to a lower status. The result was a life that was materialistically oriented. A life where things were more important than relationships.

There was another characteristic of our past orientation towards work. Too much of life was directed towards future benefits. The provisions for the children and the security for old age were to be the rewards of a lifetime of toil.

Now youth, with less confidence in the future than their parents had, are less willing to wait until the future to experience the broader aspects of life.

There is some justification for the suggestion that with our strong work orientation we have not been sufficiently sensitive to moral, social, and ethical considerations. The mark of a good job was the size of the paycheck or the retirement policy offered. Often it appeared that professions were chosen on the basis of remuneration rather than service which they rendered.

What is it that each generation should say to the other or both generations should hear from the scriptures?

Work is ordained by God and is his purpose for man. Work is rooted in creation and not in the fall. Man was created to "have dominion" and to "subdue." That sounds like work. The command to work is as clear as the command to rest. Jesus said that his Father works and he (Jesus) works. Paul dignified work by practicing his own trade and directing that those who would not share in the effort of production (work) should not share in the fruits of production (eat).

Generally speaking, the standard of living of a society is determined by the productivity of its members. The more work that is done and the greater its efficiency, the more products available. In a time when we are aware of the world-wide and even domestic need for food and shelter and health, we need to be reminded that one of the factors necessary to meet these needs is productive work. Editorials, sermons, demonstrations, and seminars may be necessary to alert the conscience and give direction, but they altogether have never made one piece of bread or one article of clothing or one cancer bandage. These are done only by work.

This suggests another biblical truth as it relates to work. All honorable work is honorable. There are different kinds of work—manual and mental. It is work to build a house. It is also work to design a house. It is work to print a book. It is also work to write it and indeed to market it. Let not him who works with men despise him who works with tools. Nor let him who works with his hands think that he who works with ideas does not really work. Having gifts differing we all contribute to the life of our community.

We need to understand the purpose of leisure. Leisure is not, as is popularly believed, the purpose of life and the reward for labor. Work is the purpose of life and leisure necessary for its effective fulfillment. Lesiure is an essential element of a life that is under the demands and pressures of work. Its value is realized when it is itself productive of recreating and broadening. There must be time to see beauty, to read great thoughts, to meditate, and to relate to others.

Work is living. To postpone living until retirement is a false concept of life and as well a foolish assumption. To assume—as the incident related early in this article seemed to suggest—that one cannot work and "praise the Lord" at the same time is not biblical. There is the ever present danger that we can become overly obsessed with work and become stooped and weary in spirit. There is also the present danger to deny the sacredness of work and to seek to escape its demands in the name of a higher happiness called leisure or a higher devotion called freedom.

This all may seem quite irrelevant when there are many who are unemployed. This may seem simplistic when so many factors nullify the efforts of production. This may seem naive when we realize that so much of our work ends up producing means of death rather than life.

I am prepared to admit all of this. These concerns are Christian concerns as well. But our basic attitude towards work is a Christian concern also. To assume that we can build a better life and "praise the Lord" more effectively by working less is a questionable assumption on both economic and biblical grounds.

---

*With apologies to non-United States readers for the nationalistic motivation on a universal subject.

"I Was in Prison . . ."

The events at Attica brought to our attention in a traumatic manner what we had known all along: the problem of crime and its attendant areas of justice and correction are extremely serious and among the most difficult in our society.

Crime continues to increase faster than the population. The average age of those involved continues to decline. Although only a minor percentage (one in five) of crimes are "solved," our courts are bogged down and justice is delayed. Our penal institutions are overcrowded and, although they often bear the hopeful title of "correctional institutions," their results belie their name, for a high percentage of those who pass through return.

Society is divided on how to meet this growing problem. Increased police power, stricter enforcement, streamlined court procedures, less sympathy for the accused, less leniency by the courts, and larger penal institutions are advocated by many.

There are those who find within our society social causes of crime. They see the need to deal with these conditions—injustice, hopelessness, and poverty—if we are going to stem the tide of crime that is inundating us.

Other observers see the issue not solely in terms of punishment and environment, but in terms of a spiritual wasteland and vacuum in our society in which respect for authority and the rights of others and a regard for moral absolutes have broken down.

The problem is a spiritual one. The solution is spiritual. Man is in rebellion against God, his fellowman, and himself. The decadence of a culture of which one of the characteristics is a disregard for the rights of others gathers momentum which can only be reversed by a deep and wide moving of the Spirit of God.

Society needs laws and their enforcement in order to be protected from those whose own standards and behavior threaten the well-being of that society. Respect for law is closely tied to the justice of the laws and their just enforcement. But the response to the present crisis by the passing of more laws, the increasing of police forces and the building of larger prisons with higher walls seems a dead-end street. This surely must be one of the lessons of Attica!

Any hope which we have must lie in a combination of the other two courses of action. It must be a combination. Neither one by itself will be an honest approach to the problem. There must be a combined concern for removing those conditions which destroy men and also for providing those spiritual resources which build character and change lives.

To deny that man is not influenced by his environment is to deny all that we teach concerning the importance of the home, discipline, nurture, and influence. To assume that there is a fair system of justice for all—rich and poor, black and white—is to leave unanswered some hard questions.

But to assume that by remedying the social causes of crime and providing justice for all we will resolve the problem, is highly questionable. One of the characteristics of the situation is the growth of crime in affluent suburbs. Criminal behavior is not really answered in terms of the social environment—it may grow faster in certain social climates and soils but its origin lies elsewhere. Its origin lies in the very nature of man. Here lies the hatred and selfishness and alienation that manifests itself in criminal behavior.

The problem which has its roots in the nature of man has its solution in the provision of God. In his offer of grace there is reconciliation and deliverance from selfishness and hatred. Man the sinner needs the experience of conversion.

The evangelical response to this insight is not found in sending Gospel Teams to jails or the announcement of a two-weeks revival to which a few of the faithful will come. Rather the answer is found in those expectations of Christ which will be one of the determining marks at the Judgment.

"I was in prison and ye came unto me."

We need not be members of a ghetto congregation to fulfil this call of Christ. There are in all of our communities men and women, youth and adult, who are or are fast becoming turned against society and are already or will be in trouble with the law and the courts. Should not individual Christians and congregations be available to our local law enforcement agencies as a resource to provide love and counsel, friendship and understanding, to those who have known little of any of these?

Is there not the need and the opportunity for a Christian community to accept into society those who are returned after years of incarceration? Would we not be fulfilling Christ's call if we would go the second mile in providing employment for such in firms where there may be more than the average Christian environment?

Is there not a call for persons with Christian motivation and understanding to choose vocations which would bear directly in a ministry to this increasingly crucial area of our community life? The opportunities for a redemptive ministry in law, social work, probation, and counseling appear unlimited.

Might this not be an opportunity for a congregation to put its life where its preaching has been and really see if God's grace and Christian love will do what we have been so piously saying it would?

Or shall we build more Atticas?

Corinth Revisited

"All Scripture is . . . profitable . . ." wrote the Apostle Paul. But has not our experience been that there have been particular Scriptures with special profit for a given situation? This which has been true in our indivdual lives has also been true in the life of the church.

When the emphasis for righteousness was on human effort either through ritual and penance, or discipline and denial, or through social ministries and good works, it was the Book of Romans that spoke to man, revealing his sinfulness and his need of justification by grace. Luther, Wesley, and Barth all found that Romans spoke with peculiar relevance to a particular time.

During the Korean war, and after, when Korean Christians were ruthlessly persecuted and life was hard and uncertain, it was the Book of Revelation that became meaningful to them. I understand that this book was memorized by many and its message of hope and God's final triumph sustained them in those difficult days.

If the character of the times has a bearing on the significance of Scripture, we may do well to turn to Paul's letters to the Corinthians. We are today living in a Corinthian culture. It affects all our lives and our values. Many new Christians have been converted from this culture. It is to this culture that the church of our day is called to minister.

It is a sensate culture, sensate not just as in sex, but in the broader sense of feeling. It is an emotional age. Happiness and pleasure become the highest good—the goal of life.

I usually go home for lunch. Part of my noon routine is to tune in the noonday news on CBS at 12:25. One day I tuned in either earlier than usual or left the TV on longer than the news and I got the beginning or the end of one of those situation melodramas called "Search for Tomorrow" or "Love of Life."

As I pieced the situation together it appeared that the son of the family had not returned home during the night. The family fears were that he had eloped with a girl of whom they did not approve. As they shared the fears and concerns over morning coffee (any other time of day it would have been cocktails) one of the members—I believe the grandmother—said, "If they are really happy, I guess that is all that really matters."

And she spoke for many. For whether we eat or drink, work or play, marry or give in marriage, we do all to the glory of happiness. Our age lives by its emotions. Our feelings are our guide. How we feel rather than how we think about a situation determines our actions. This becomes evident in flexible moral standards. It results in impetuous acts. It determines the pattern of life. It is evident in the lack of discipline and the disregard for authority. It finds its ultimate expression in our drug culture and the emotion-packed activities of mass gatherings or intimate groups. We live by our hearts rather than our heads.

We are all affected by this spirit of the times—some more than others. As Christians we are influenced by it. It determines the pattern and expectation of Christian experience. The Christian faith becomes highly subjective and becomes an escape from reality. There is more to the significance of the terms "trip" and "high" when used in the Christian context than a concern for modernity of language. It suggests that the Christian faith is essentially a means to a higher state of happiness.

The church at Corinth reflected in their church life the age and culture from which they had been saved. Their confusion as it related to sex, their lack of decorum in worship, their love of freedom and doing their own thing, and their fascination with spiritual gifts reflected a certain culturalization of their Christian experience.

Paul was concerned for their maturity. He did not discount the grace which they had experienced. He rejoiced in this. But he was aware of their immaturity—their carnal spirit. He spent much of the first letter in a labored effort to instruct these Christians in the implications and meaning of the Christian life. The areas he covered sound extremely modern.

He presented to them a Christian view on marriage and on sex. The obsession and degradation of sex in a culture can have varied reaction on the part of those who have been converted out of this environment. It can be one of accommodation in which the moral patterns of society are rationalized into becoming the patterns of the Christian community. Or sex can be repudiated and the drive denied and a type of asceticism advocated. Paul escaped both of these, although his sense of urgency was reflected in his position on the assuming of family responsibilities. He recognized the legitimacy and sacredness of a person's sexuality. He maintained the sanctity of the marriage relationship as the expression of this part of human personality.

He was concerned with order, discipline, and respect for authority. The unrepentant member needed to be disciplined. The conduct in worship and in the communion service called for Paul's attention. The receiving and the use of gifts were not for the individual but for the church and were to be used with understanding. Emotions were to be subject to the intelligence. Man was both head and heart.

Paul was concerned about the fruit of the Spirit. In this very earthy epistle Paul inserted the beautiful hymn on love. This hymn is not on lyrical and romantic love but on practical love—love on the horizontal—love that cares and gives and suffers. The ultimate expression of Christian experience is Christian character and not Christian gifts.

There is ever the peril that an emphasis upon experience results in experience becoming the beginning and the end. A society immersed in feeling is in danger of carrying into their Christian life a strong commitment to the emotional. Christ essentially becomes another means to a higher happiness.

This tendency comes through when we paraphrase the Beatitudes to read "Happy is the man . . ." It manifests itself when our Christian worship is predominantly subjective and horizonal. It comes through when our own experience and the freedom we sense disregards the brother's conscience or the church's mind.

Let us be grateful for the new moving of the Spirit. Let us share with Paul his gratitude for the grace of God that ministers to all men of all cultures. And while sharing his joy, we also do well to share his concern.

There's a Bit of
the Pharisee Around

No one I know wants to be called a Pharisee. No matter where you place the accent it does not sound good. The original bearers of the name owe their claim to fame to their violent opposition to Jesus and to his teaching.

I doubt if the contemporaries of the Pharisees would have regarded them in as unfavorable a light as we. A Pharisee may not have been a popular choice as a fishing companion, but I suspect that he was generally considered to be a good person and certainly religious.

They did have some things to their credit. They were orthodox. They were men of the Word. They took seriously the Bible and many of its demands—Sabbath observance, clean and unclean, tithing, fastings, and prayer. They were zealous—indeed evangelistic, traversing ". . . sea and land to make a single proselyte . . ."

But they came under the judgment of Jesus, and no other group in Jesus' day came under such scathing denunciation as did the Pharisees.

What was the matter?

They were naive in their understanding of sin. They equated sin with overt acts and righteousness with outward forms. Jesus saw that sin was deeper than rules and laws could reach. He saw beneath their moral and ritualistic facade those sins which do not submit to rules and regulations—pride, selfishness, hatred, and envy. Jesus described this fact in graphic terms. He called them "whitewashed tombs."

They had an inadequate understanding of the Scriptures. They followed the letter and missed the message. Jesus observed that they searched the Scriptures "because you think that in them you have eternal life; and it is they that bear witness to me, yet you refuse to come to me that you may have life." So devoted to the Scriptures and so blind!

They were selective in their obedience to Scripture. This was all the more serious because they chose to obey the less important. Jesus did give them credit for certain of their practices but censored them because they failed to observe the more weighty "matters of the law, justice, and mercy, and faith."

They were deeply concerned about their "righteousness" and overly impressed by it. They wanted to be different. The Pharisee who came to the temple thanked God that he was not like other people. The virtues he practiced and the vices from which he refrained were foremost in his thinking. He was impressed and he thanked God.

They were for law and for justice—especially as it related to the other man's sins—Sabbath breakers, blasphemers, and adulterers. Had Jesus preached against these sins only, the Pharisees would have been his strong supporters. But Jesus spoke against all sin, including theirs, and they proved him right. They killed him.

They revealed little of compassion and mercy. Probably no other characteristic of their life was in such marked contrast to Jesus. The keeping of the Sabbath was more important than the restoring of sight to a man blind. An ox in a ditch took precedence over a man in need. The enforcement of law was more important than the redemption of a woman. Those who because of occupation or poverty or disposition did not keep the law as did the Pharisees were regarded as "sinners" and "common people."

One could hope that Pharisaism has long since died out. Surely we flee Pharisaism as a plague. Not so. This type of religious devotion is too natural to the heart of man. It hovers over congregations like a deadly fog and settles in at the slightest opportunity. I venture that the sins of the Pharisees—legalism, pride, hypocrisy, judging, selfishness, and hatred—do more to nullify our efforts of evangelism than the so-called sins of worldliness and of the flesh that may be present among us.

I sometimes hear among evangelicals overtones of the Pharisee's prayer, "God, I thank thee that I am not like other men . . ." We place great emphasis upon outward conduct and morality and piety. The assumption, spoken or unspoken, is that if we are good enough, these evidences of devotion will be honored by God, and sinners will be convicted.

But I propose that it is not the Pharisee's prayer which we should be praying, but the publican's: "God be merciful to me a sinner." Nor is it out of order to point out that near the end of his ministry the Apostle Paul spoke of himself as the chief of sinners *in the present tense* (I Tim. 1:15).

There needs to be and will be that difference in the life of a Christian, but it is the difference of grace. A difference that comes from being in Christ. It works from the inside out. And with all this difference Christians are still real people—people who cast a shadow when they walk and who bleed when they are cut—people who are genuine and honest in their claims of victory and defeat, and in the admission of need.

This trace of Pharisaism is also evident in our value structure. We do well in our keeping of certain commandments—those that can be committed to rules and regulations. Most of us are respectable, moral, and law abiding. We manage to stay out of jail. Many do fairly well in prayers, and tithing, and going to the "temple."

But those "weightier" matters of compassion and caring and mercy and justice are too often missing. I recall a pastor's account of his being criticized for his failure to "preach on sin." So, one Sunday he preached on sin—sin(s) in the common usage of the term. He relates how disturbed he was by the favorable comments he received. For these favorable comments came from those of his congregation whose general attitude was judgmental and rigid. In their lives was lacking the compassion and caring that won for our Lord the title, "friend of publicans and sinners."

This brings us to another trace of Pharisaism among us—a lack of compassion—an absence of really caring. This is not the same as evangelism or a passion for souls. There is an evangelism without compassion. The Pharisees had that. Too many of us and too many congregations lack the ability to care deeply, to get close, to identify; there are just too many things in our religious life that are more important than people.

There are innumerable congregations committed to evangelism. The messages are evangelistic. Concerted prayers are made for a moving of God. They schedule special meetings, community visitation, and prayer vigils. Little happens. They try harder— more prayers and new methods. Little happens.

I have an intimation that if we would get quiet enough Christ would say some of the things to us and to our congregations that he said to the Pharisees. And if we would have, as did that Pharisee who met Christ on the road to Damascus, a greater sense of God's grace and our need of it, and a lesser sense of our righteousness, revival would come and with it a moving of God resulting in those who are outside coming in. And we, who are now known as "the friends of holiness," would then be known as "the friends of sinners," which, after all, is not such a bad title.

Unlimited Liability

Jesus reminded his followers of three groups which were to be the focus of their love.

"I say to you, love your enemies and pray for those who persecute you . . ."

In reply to a scribe's inquiry, Jesus replied that "you shall love your neighbor as yourself."

In the intimate conversation with his disciples just prior to his crucifixion Jesus gave his own commandment—"This is my commandment, that you love one another as I have loved you."

It seems obvious that there is an added dimension to a Christian's love for his fellow Christian that goes beyond the high demands of neighbor love. A very proper question would be, "How has Christ loved us?" Any Sunday school child knows the answer. "He laid down his life for us." Jesus explains that this is the ultimate in love: "Greater love has no man than this, that a man lay down his life for his friends."

Few of us are called to experience literally this giving of our life for a brother. But there are those daily opportunities granted to us as Christians to express this same quality of love.

I recently heard the term "unlimited liability" used to describe the kind of love that should be experienced within the Christian community. The natural place for this to be expressed is within the congregation. Time would be well spent if congregations would examine the meaning and the day to day outworking of this quality of love within the life of a congregation—loving one another as Christ loves us.

This understanding is an essential element in evangelism. The love of God and our love for God will send us out. Our love for one another will draw men in. Where else, pray tell, can a person go where he can experience this quality of love? Where else can one go where he will experience this unlimited liability—no matter what happens, underneath will be the everlasting arms—of the brethren?

Anxiety

Leighton Ford has made an interesting and, I believe, a perceptive observation in relation to man's basic anxieties*—death, guilt, and meaninglessness.

Dr. Ford states that for ancient man death was his chief anxiety; for the Middle Ages it was guilt; for moderns it is meaninglessness.

Ancient cultures met this anxiety of death with the formation of a belief or hope of an after-life. The Greeks held that death released the spirit from the restriction of the body to enter immortality. The Egyptians carefully prepared their dead for the life to come. Indeed the early Christian Fathers, with their emphasis on eternal life, give support to the observation that for the ancients death was their deep anxiety.

Martin Luther, with his doctrine of forgiveness—justification by faith; Saint Anselm, with his interpretation of the atonement as satisfaction; and indeed the traditional equating of salvation as forgiveness represents the Middle Ages and subsequent generations' anxiety of guilt.

Modern man—philosophers, writers, and artists—reflect the anxiety of our times as one of meaninglessness. Man has only an existence. His life has no real purpose or destiny. Our society through its culture expresses this same lack of meaning. The drug culture (pot for the youth and alcohol for their parents) can only be correctly understood and realistically faced when it is recognized as having its roots in man's anxiety—meaninglessness and emptiness. Despair and cynicism on the one hand, and self-serving hedonism and violence on the other, are fruits of this anxiety.

These are understandable anxieties—death, guilt and meaninglessness. Man has eternity stamped upon him. Obedience was his original calling. These combined to give purpose to his life. It is understandable that their absence haunts man's soul—individual and corporate.

These anxieties which, as suggested, have found unique expression in particular periods of history, are also a part of our own experience. A sense of guilt, a dread and fear of death, and a lack of meaning are experiences of our lives. Since these are a result of man's sin, we do well to look for their answer in God's provision.

Guilt

The death and resurrection of Christ affect man's guilt in two ways—they produce guilt and remove it.

What the law was to the Jews in making them aware of sin, the cross with the resurrection are to man today. Men may argue with standards of ethics and morality, and justify their actions and lives, as an increasing number are, without a sense of sin or guilt. But it is difficult to argue with love. This was the approach of Paul when he found himself in Corinth—a sensate and immoral culture. He did not preach the law. He preached Jesus Christ and him crucified.

A biblical sense of guilt is not so much that we have disobeyed the law but that man has refused Christ. We recall the response at Pentecost when Peter pointed out to that large crowd that this

Jesus whom they had crucified God had raised up. Their cry, "What must we do to be saved," was based upon their awareness of Christ crucified and risen rather than upon moral and ethical shortcomings.

Let it be known far and wide that the purpose of Christ's coming and his choice of the cross was to save sinners. Let it also be known that with an investment such as this, no repentant sinner will be turned away; no penitent backslider will be refused. The cross and the empty tomb are irrefutable proof that God's love is greater than all my sins or yours.

Meaninglessness

The book of Ecclesiastes should have significance for our day. The writer—successful, refined, educated, powerful, and wealthy—found life empty and meaningless. So like modern man! Man's efforts have no purpose. As an individual he has no real worth.

To such a condition the cross and the empty tomb speak. They speak of man's worth. They speak of man's individuality and identity.

The one who loved us with a Calvary love is the risen Lord. It is for him we now live. His cause is our life and work. Its victory is assured. He is the companion of the road. His presence brings joy. His companionship warms the heart. He stands beside the bed of pain and sits with us in the hour of grief. We are important in his plans.

Death

The ultimate expression of meaninglessness is death. But the final answer to meaninglessness is the resurrection of Christ.

The question of Job is still man's great concern. "If a man die, shall he live again?" The empty tomb declares that not only shall man live again but in that life he will maintain his identity. The resurrection is not a general immortality but the continuation of individuality.

We need not become bogged down with curious questions of means and method. Paul in his great chapter on the resurrection (I Cor. 15) gives us a sketch of that life which is to come—where mortality and corruption will be no more but where identity and individuality will continue forevermore.

Christ's tomb was not empty as proof of immortality. The tomb was empty because God gives resurrection. He does this because what he has created is good and we who are created in his image are of value to him.

This truth is both a great hope and a sobering fact. Inexorably tied with individuality is responsibility. Beyond death is the resurrection. Beyond the open tomb is the judgment seat.

---

*He gives due credit to Paul Tillich for this concept of anxieties.

The Mark of *Authenticity*

Thomas did not graduate at the head of the class. Nor would he have been voted "the one most likely to succeed." The notation in the "yearbook" results in a nickname being given—"The Doubter." And it has stuck. Thomas, the twin, has been known as "Doubting Thomas."

We have been a little hard on Thomas and, I suspect, rather unfair. What he wanted to know was, "Is this one whom my friends have identified as the Christ the real One?" After all, Jesus had warned that false christs would come—christs who would show great signs and wonders. But Thomas was wise enough to know that the authentic Christ would bear nail prints in his hands and a scar of a spear in his side. And if he was going to commit himself he wanted to be certain.

Thomas was a wise man. "Except I see and feel I will not believe." The number of modern Thomases are legion. They search for something in which to believe. They look to someone to follow. But they insist on authenticity. Too often what they see, what they hear, and what they are offered lack this mark of the real thing. They do not see the marks of the crucifixion in the body of Christ—the church.

The church has discovered the Second Commandment and has sought to minister to men in their need and suffering. But it must be said that not all of this ministry has borne the marks of authenticity. Not all the hands outstretched to help were nail scarred.

The motivation for service and the spirit in which it is ministered may vary—self-fulfillment, the appeasing of guilt, and an attitude of paternalism. Those on the receiving end can detect the motives. Doors have closed and are closing because this ministry did not carry the marks of authenticity. They were not genuinely Christian.

What has been said about ministries is also true of evangelism. The message and the method need to bear the marks of the genuine. There must be more to preaching than orthodoxy and shibboleths. There must be more to witnessing than zeal and a reservoir of texts. The message and the method must bear the marks of the nails.

How does the mark of authenticity express itself in the Christian's life and the Christian message? What does it mean to preach "Jesus Christ crucified"? What does it mean to be "crucified with Him"? What does it mean to be the Body of Christ?

It surely means that in our proclamation and in our living we see the cross and Christ's death as crucial in God's dealing with the individual's sin and his guilt. But the cross has more than judicial significance. It is the way God deals with evil. This is the way his church faces life and confronts evil.

When the Christian and the church accept suffering and absorb hatred and identify with those who suffer and are oppressed, they will bear the marks of this suffering—the nail prints will be there. The authenticating marks of the true church—if it is indeed the Body of Christ—are not correctness of doctrine nor beauty of ritual, they are not social service nor evangelism, they are not miracles nor growth. The marks of the body of Christ are those of the resurrected Christ with the nail prints in his hands and the scar in his side—marks of redemptive love and redemptive suffering.

Jesus came near enough so that Thomas could verify. And herein lies a lesson. The authenticity of the gospel and the Christian life is not verified from afar but in relationships and in closeness. These marks will be evident primarily in the usual and the common experiences and duties of our lives. In our rejection of power and self seeking. In our response to evil and hatred through love. It is our identification with man in his humanity and his sin.

Unless our service and evangelism and witnessing bear the marks of authenticity they will be less than effective. But if there is stamped upon our message and our lives the print of the nails and the scar of the spear, there will be that note of authenticity which will elicit in our day the response: "My Lord, and My God."

The Bible Is No Fetish

The account of the temptations of Jesus in the wilderness is one of the better known gospel narratives. Detailed in two of the Gospels and referred to in another, this fascinating account could have come only from the Master himself.

Well known to every one acquainted with the account is the method Christ used to counter the temptations and thwart Satan's efforts. In each instance Christ turned to the Scriptures. This fact has been often pointed out and emphasized as a resource and method available to the Christian.

So it is. However, the impression often left is that there is something magical about the quoting of Scripture which "neutralizes" the devil's efforts and breaks the power of his temptation. This is not the lesson to be learned from the temptation narrative. The power of the Word of God—the Scriptures—is not a magical power but a reasonable one.

The Scriptures which Jesus used were pertinent and reasonable answers to Satan's suggestions. Each Scripture was appropriate to the particular temptation. This is evidence that Christ did not rely on a few memorized verses which he could recall on short notice (in fact, the Scriptures which Jesus knew did not have "verses"). Rather, he had a reservoir of biblical knowledge which supported and enlightened him. This knowledge enabled him to detect the logical and attractive temptations of Satan and to resist them.

Our own strength to resist is closely related to our knowledge of the Word of God. How else can one detect the subtlety of Satan's logic? How else does one counter Satan's own use of Scripture? Not by a few memory verses! Rather, by a broad and deep knowledge of Scripture which brings to bear upon the issues of life the eternal truths of God's revealed truth.

The Holy Scriptures which are able to make one wise unto salvation are also able to make one wise unto the logic of Satan.

The New Immorality

You thought I was going to write about lust, didn't you? You are right. Only this time it is a five-letter word. It is spelled M-O-N-E-Y.

I grew up believing that gambling was one of the baser sins. It destroyed character, wrecked homes, squandered savings, led to violence, and was detrimental to the common good. Society seemed to concur. Gambling was forbidden by statute.

Times have changed. What was a vice is now a virtue. What was the basis for a police raid is now the occasion for televised pageantry. What was once restricted to back rooms is now on billboards and front pages. It is no longer called gambling. It is now "the lottery." But like the proverbial "rose by any other name" it smells just the same.

In more and more states man's fascination with chance and his desire for sudden wealth have provided a temptation the state could not resist. So the lottery has become a means of additional revenue for the ever-empty public coffers and has been dignified as a patriotic duty.

The ultimate test of rightness or wrongness is not the votes of the legislatures or a referendum by the people. Nor is it determined by whether or not it is permitted or even encouraged by the state. Rather it must be measured against biblical values and Christian obedience.

Gambling is a form of stealing. Gambling is to stealing what dueling is to murder. In each case each participant supposedly has an equal chance but in each case one loses and one wins. In the case of dueling, the loser is dead. In the case of gambling, the winner takes all, giving nothing of equivalent value in return. Where in stealing he took it by stealth or by force, in gambling he took it by chance.

The Apostle's word to the Ephesians: "Let him that stole, steal no more . . ." must take on new meaning and new relevance to the Christian today. Stealing is now legal and in fact encouraged. It is not called thievery. It is called "the lottery."

Gambling is an expression of covetousness. The New Testament Greek word translated "covetousness" means "to wish to have more." The word does not carry that shade of meaning we have long associated with it which relates to "wanting that which belongs to another." Rather it means simply "to want more."

The Bible is downright hard on covetousness. Jesus said, "Beware of covetousness (wanting more)." Paul in Colossians 3:5 lists it with "fornication, uncleanness, inordinate affection, and evil concupiscense." But he goes one step further with the sin of covetousness by adding the phrase "which is idolatry."

Idolatry in the Bible receives particularly harsh judgment. It is the ultimate sin. It reflects the transfer of loyalty and worship from God to another—the idol. Paul is saying that man's wanting more is the new idolatry—not a graven image, but engraved certificates.

It is this lust for more that feeds the lottery and is itself fed by the lottery. Just as state-supported prostitution would not make it right, so state-supported and encouraged gambling does not make it right. It is still stealing and is still an expression of covetousness.

Gambling is a betrayal of stewardship. A cardinal teaching of the Scriptures is that what man has he has been given and he holds it as a trust. The manner in which a Christian carries out this trust of time, means, and abilities is a crucial test of one's faith.

Obviously, this applies to money. Nor is our trust satisfied by merely giving the tithe. Our trust is for the ten tenths and carries over to what we often inaccurately describe as "that which we have left"—meaning for ourselves.

One does not need to "stretch a point" to conclude that stewardship has something to say about gambling. Moth and rust, against which Jesus warned, are considerably better risks and have greater permanence than the predetermined chance of the lottery. Gambling lays up treasure neither on earth or in heaven.

Gambling reflects the human sickness. The selfishness which seeks gain out of proportion to contribution made, the boredom which seeks synthetic and self-destructive thrills, and depravity which seeks to profit from the losses of others are all symptoms of this illness.

This sickness is further reflected in a society that seeks to dignify these defects in the human family by making them appear worthy and noble. Indeed, society encourages this malignancy and will in the end be destroyed by it.

There is little hope that the national trend towards the use of lotteries to supplement public income will be reversed. When moral and ethical values have become warped, the lottery is too attractive to both the individual citizen and hard-pressed public officials to anticipate its early demise.

This phenomenon is another piece of evidence that the Christian lives in the world but dare not be of it. This becomes another choice which a Christian is called to make. It is one more evidence that what may be approved by man or the state is not necessarily approved by God.

There are persuasive and reasonable reasons why gambling—the lottery—should not be permitted, reasons purely rational and pragmatic. We have not turned to these. The Christian has reasons

beyond the pragmatic. Gambling runs counter to all that the
Christian faith stands for and against. The biblical call is loud and
clear to us who bear the name Christian. Have nothing to do with
this new immorality!

Glamour Missions

Letters bearing appeals for financial support of religious and
benevolent causes tug at our heart strings and pull at our purse
strings.

It does something inside of me to open an appeal letter, see the
pleading eyes of a hungry child, and read of desperate need for
funds in an area where the Spirit of God is reportedly working in a
special way, and then to toss this appeal into my waste basket. The
inability to respond to all of these appeals is obvious. But how does
one determine which are worthy of support and which are not?

One of the annual appeals which I found difficult to discard was
from a well-known midwest benevolent institution. I never failed
to be touched by the familiar photograph which appeared on their
literature and the well-known phrase, "He's not heavy, father, he's
my brother." Perhaps it is because the editor's home has special-
ized in sons, or perhaps it is because a church leader, highly
regarded by me, stated that he always gives to this institution, that
I have always found it difficult to turn down this appeal.

My problem will not be quite so difficult this year. A recent news
release reports that in a recent year this organization received four
times more in contributions than was used in carrying out its
purpose. This fact does not suggest dishonest or unethical practices in the usual understanding of those terms. It does indicate, if
this report is true, that this organization's need of my support is
not very great.

It is difficult to determine the integrity and the Christian character of a ministry by the contents of a letter, the appearance of a
brochure, or the message of a radio program.

A radio ministry in a midwestern state capitol had through the
years been recognized as a strong evangelical voice. The founder
died. The ministry, including facilities, the listening audience,
and the mailing list was left to the daughter. Her husband was the

radio voice, i.e., he was until she became suspicious and had him followed on one of his evangelistic campaigns. Her suspicions were verified. She divorced him and hired another man to be the voice of the ministry. This in fact multiplied the "ministry" since the ex-husband took the mailing list with him and established another "ministry" in a distant state. The replacement speaker on the original broadcast had the same last name as the ex-husband for reasons which seem obvious, at least to me.

Assuredly not all organizations using the mails for their appeals, nor the radio as their media, are unworthy of support. But how does one distinguish between the worthy and the unworthy? Some are divisive in their mission work, building on the work of reputable and established works. Others fail to meet the tests of good stewardship because of inefficient operations and high overhead. Some use commercial fund-raising organizations who keep a high percentage of the funds contributed by sincere and sacrificial donors. Even once reputable organizations change character as leadership changes or the ministry becomes the property of the family of the founder.

This becomes quite relevant when the mails bring their many appeals (I recently received eight identical letters from what most of us would regard as a worthy ministry). What is the response of Christian concern and stewardship to these appeals?

It is at a time like this that I am aware of another of the benefits of my denominational association. I could investigate those appeals which seem worthy, obtain financial reports, secure first hand reports of their ministry, become acquainted with the leadership at the administrative and at the board levels, and thus determine if their ministry is divisive or supportive in the area where they work. I could learn if it is an individual or family oriented program, and when I am satisified that they are worthy of support could make my contribution. But my denominational identity answers all of these questions for me. Those who administer the several ministries of the church are my brethren, the board members who supervise are members of our congregations or pastors in our churches.

No organization is perfect and the more we know about it the more obvious are some of the shortcomings. But those "wonderful" ministries about which we read and hear through their promotional literature and radio broadcasts are so because we know so little about them. Usually the glamor of a program is in indirect proportion to our knowledge of it.

We are not suggesting that all non-denominational work is unworthy of support. There are ministries that have integrity and command respect. There are some whose leadership we know very well and respect. Their work is supportive of those programs we support as a denomination.

But I am concerned about these ministries of which we know so little but which seem so worthy. Most of us would not purchase real estate on the basis of a four-color brochure and a smooth talking stranger. We should be just as discriminating and just as conscientious with the Lord's money as with our own.

All of this helps me solve the problem of what to do when the appeals come. I discard these letters a little easier and support the denominational needs a little more.

In Praise of Romance

The 14th of February is dedicated to romance. Anniversaries and other special days have their romantic overtones but no day is so unabashedly romantic as is Valentine's Day.

One will not find the day listed among the church's Holy Days. This is understandable, although it is really *Saint* Valentine's Day. We are not suggesting that it be placed on a par with Easter and Christmas. But should not the day have equal billing with Mother's Day and Father's Day? I have heard mothers extolled on Mother's Day and fathers reminded on Father's Day in Sunday school openings and in the worship hour. I have, to my knowledge, never heard a sermon in praise of romance delivered on the Sunday nearest to Valentine's Day.

Maybe romance is not that of which sermons are made, but it is that of which good marriages consist. The virtues of motherhood and the strength of fatherhood will both be found wanting if the quality of romance is absent in the marriage relationship.

Pity the wife from whose heart romance has fled, who at this time of year does not hunt for a lace-trimmed card with sentiments she feels, but cannot quite bring herself to say. And now, having found just the card, she places it where her husband will find it, and, if possible, will watch from an unobserved vantage point as he opens and reads it.

Shame on the husband who no longer lets himself be carried away into buying one of those heart-shaped boxes of candy—

where the box costs more than the candy, and who then watches with a school boy shyness as she opens the box and says, "You shouldn't have done it!" And both know deep in their hearts that he should have. Maybe it's a pretty dress they could not afford— except on Valentine's Day—or a meal in a restaurant with cloth napkins, candles at each table, and tables just for two.

Of such things and others is romance made. How tragic the marriage from which it has fled. How sad the home where the eyes do not light up at the sight of the other or the heartbeat quicken at the touch of the hand. How irreparably deprived are those children of a home where the fire of romance has been allowed to go out and words of endearment are never heard and acts of affection are never seen.

But marriages cannot survive on romance alone. Romance is too fragile to by itself weather the storms which beat upon the marriage. One of the causes of our mounting marriage casualties is that romance is seen as the foundation of marriage. Our society has asked it to bear more than it is able, and in the process both marriage and romance become casualties. Of itself it is an inadequate base.

Unless we are prepared to resort to "planned" marriages, as is the pattern in other cultures, romantic love will continue to be the initial and powerful catalyst which will bring a man and a maiden to the marriage altar. Romantic love will be that which will cause them not only to be willing but to be eager to forsake all others and to accept the responsibilities and disciplines of the marriage state.

For the long pull more than romance is needed. The foundation from the biblical perspective is *faithfulness.* A stable marriage must be undergirded by a commitment to each other that is binding regardless of the ebb and flow of feelings and the variations of circumstances. Faithfulness means that there is no room for second thoughts, that there is no going back, for deep within each partner all bridges have been burned and all options destroyed. It is on such a foundation that marriages are built, and such a foundation is required for their survival.

The Christian marriage has an added quality. To faithfulness is added Christian love—*agape* love. Romantic love is partly self-centered and self-motivated. *Apage* love is "other-centered." Romantic love is based on the qualities and virtues and worth seen in the other person which will bring enrichment to the life of the admirer. *Agape* love is based on Christ's caring love expressed in and through us. It is kind and longsuffering. It goes the second mile. It forgives and heals. It is unilateral—given regardless of response. But *agape* love, in itself, is not an adequate basis for marriage. It is an essential ingredient in its survival and its health, but we do not marry on the basis of *agape* love.

Marriages held together by faithfulness alone may be little more than a legal contract or an economic convenience. Add to this *agape* love and one has added qualities of caring and respect. But, in truth, this adds no quality different than that which should characterize the relationship of Christians with each other.

Give me a marriage founded upon faithfulness, supported by *agape* love, and lighted by romance and I will show you a relationship which is the envy of angels and the joy of the whole earth. It is from such marriages that children rise up and call their parents blessed.

Romance is a fragile thing. It needs the constant attention of husband and wife. It will die in the pressure of a too busy life and the aridity of thoughtlessness and selfishness. It needs the kind word, the affectionate glance, the unexpected act of thoughtfulness, the evening alone, and the added pressure to the held hand. Romance, like man, does not live by bread alone.

Romance transforms the vows of faithfulness from an obligation to a privilege. It stops the "second thoughts" before they begin and defuses the wayward glance.

Faithfulness, *agape* love, and romance are a holy trinity which will make the marriage relationship a touch of heaven on earth. We need a renewed emphasis upon this trinitarian doctrine. We have been paying a tragic price for its neglect.

Redemptive and Supportive

I heard of a church leader, in a denomination which takes the obligations of church membership seriously, who was opposed to revival meetings because, he said, "People would be converted. They would want to join the church. And there would be all kinds of problems because they do not know the rules."

Now, before we censor this brother too severely we would do well to be certain that there is not a similar reluctance on our part to relate to those who have not lived by the rules.

In some communities this may mean every other home on the block. In other communities it will be one home in three or four.

These are homes with a history of divorce and remarriage. The greater the commitment to and involvement in evangelism, the more crucial becomes our attitude towards this home in three or four.

Do we believe that the offer of salvation is a valid option for those with a complicated marital history? Does the "whosoever" include those whose philosophy of marriage included an escape clause which they chose to use and then decided to try again? Was Jesus serious in his conversation with the woman at the well or was he making pious small talk?

The response to the above questions would be almost unanimous: The "whosoever" of the gospel invitation includes all. There would be almost as much unanimity that it is the church's obligation to make its "whosoever" as broad as the gospel's.

There is less agreement as we move on in search of answers to questions which naturally and logically follow. What is the nature of the response to the gospel on the part of those with a background of divorce and remarriage? How do we understand the strong biblical statements regarding this relationship and what does God expect as the response to his grace? Is this a question that each person must answer within himself and between himself and God, or does the church have a word of counsel and understanding?

Closely related to the question of what God requires is the question of what the church expects. There needs to be a common understanding if there is to be acceptance by the congregation. There needs to be a biblical and Christian frame of reference from which the pastor counsels and the congregation supports and receives.

An easy way and an all too common approach is to assume that this is a matter "between you and God." "Do you feel God has forgiven you?" Ultimately there must be this kind of personal experience. But it is not a case of the church standing by as a spectator to this spiritual struggle. The church is involved not only in prayer but in seeking to understand the biblical messages, the essence of the sin, the nature of repentance, and the extent of God's grace and in sharing these insights with the couple.

Repentance keeps cropping up because forgiveness is involved. Of what does one, in the situation with which we are concerned, repent? What evidence does the church expect that the repentance is valid? In less complicated cases of infidelity the answer may be obvious. But there are those other cases that do not submit to simple answers. There will be situations where the present marriage is by all standards a happier marriage and a more satisfactory family life than the earlier one. There are children loved and wanted. What is the real meaning of repentance in this situation?

If the church is to be serious about evangelism we need to find a brotherhood concensus on what is the redemptive message to this one home in three and what is required for full fellowship in the body.

The church's concern with those involved in situations of re-marriage is only one part of the issue. Equally as urgent a concern is the responsibility to the families within the fellowship—supporting the present marriages, assisting in family relationships, and pre-paring the youth for responsible and meaningful marriage.

Several observations may be in order.

First: Christian marriage is increasingly taking on a unique meaning. It is more than a marriage solemnized by the church or entered into by a man and woman who are Christians. Rather it is based on the concept of a covenant between a man and a woman that is a life-long union sealed by God—"Whom God hath joined together."

Whatever may be the implications for those marriages which are not entered into with this understanding, it means that the Chris-tian understanding of marriage is more than a societal or cultural institution and its entering into and its living out is more than a legal arrangement. Marriage is God-ordained and God-fashioned.

The situation which highlights this distinction is that the understanding of marriage in our society no longer carries the biblical standards which have for generations guided society's pattern of marriage. No cataloging of present practices is needed to confirm the point that the idea of marriage has departed far from its biblical moorings.

Second: The church must become a community of support. One of the problems of marriages is the isolation in which the couple lives or the destructive influences of that community with which they identify. Christian marriages need the support of a Christian community.

This support is realized when the church and the congregation take seriously the events that relate to marriage and the family. It is realized when the congregation is alert to the needs and problems that bear upon the marriage. It is realized when through teaching and preaching those sins—such as selfishness, impatience, and the lustful eye—which threaten marriages are pointed out. It is real-ized when materialism and the right to happiness are shown to be perilous to marriage. It is realized when there is openness and candor which enables needs to be shared and failures to be acknowledged.

As the church relates evangelistically to society and receives into its fellowship those with a background of marital involvements, the need to be supportive of the Christian concept of marriage increases. But the urgency is not based only on the premise of outreach. The pressure and influence of society upon our homes and our marriages is very real. Whatever thought is given to being redemptive to those without, it needs to be matched by how we can be supportive to those within.

Let's Not Be Weary

Perhaps we need a rest—a time to catch our breath. Maybe it is pure and simple discouragement. Whatever it is, society as a whole and the church in particular has been deemphasizing the obligation to become involved in the relief of human suffering and a ministry to human need.

We are tired of words like integration and racial tension. The terms poverty, malnutrition, Appalachia, and illiteracy no longer challenge us as they once did. Population explosion and pollution no longer carry the call for response.

The call to serve in Voluntary Service, PAX, and even the more traditional missionary ministries has lost its appeal. Mission hospitals function on a part time schedule dependent upon availability of personnel.

The church has turned inward. Experience has replaced service as the essence of the Christian faith. Love has become a feeling in contrast to a ministry. The small group or the mass rally is where the action is. What social outreach there is is related closely to these experience oriented expressions and more often than not relates to the problem of drugs.

This swing of the pendulum could be explained in several ways. The history of the Christian church could probably be written from the perspective of the swing of the pendulum. There are always corrective reactions at work to pull the church back from what is interpreted as an over emphasis.

Perhaps we were all too optimistic. We assumed that laws and money could solve the problem at the government level. We assumed that dedicated service and love and a little money could go a long way towards meeting needs at any level. But the problems were too complex and too deeply rooted. Discouragement led to disillusionment and disillusionment to disengagement. We decided to contribute to the solution by looking out for ourselves and our own.

It is possible that our inner resources for service were inadequate. We were spiritually undercapitalized for the demanding ministry to which we were committed. Christian ministry must be motivated by more than the rewards of success. There must be an inner motivation that accepts the cross as the Christian's reward.

And so the pendulum has swung. Experience is now where it is at. To the degree that this emphasis is biblical and does not become an end in itself, it is for the good. Christianity deals with the ultimate questions of life—being, death, meaning, sin, grace, guilt, and hope. No amount of religious activity, be it ritual or service or evangelistic effort, will provide the answers to these questions.

But when experience is an end in itself, or when it needs increasing heights of esctasy to satisfy the person's needs, the Christian faith has been perverted.

The Lord of the church characterized his ministry with that of a servant. He went around doing good. The all night prayer vigils or the mountain top retreat did not raise him beyond touching the leprous man or healing the epileptic child. He was careful to keep the two commandments—love of God and love of neighbor—together.

A Mission Field

Our prisons are one of the major problems of our society and a major opportunity for the church. Crime is increasing, the courts are backlogged, and our prisons crowded. There must be a better way to respond to this problem than meting out more severe sentences and building more and larger prisons.

What can be done to deal redemptively with individuals whose present lifestyle is leading them to confrontation with the law and incarceration? What alternatives does society have to incarceration? What can communities do to receive back into their lives those who have paid the laws' demands? Society is not doing very well—on the whole—in any of these three areas. Does not the church have the resources to move into this mission field? As geographical frontiers disappear, we need eyes to see other frontiers to which the church and Christians can minister and should.

The Christian understands the nature of man and the power of sin. He should be aware that "but for the grace of God, there go I." He is conscious of the spiritual resources which are beyond the human and the social. He understands failure. He maintains hope which never writes a man off. He has the resources of a praying and caring community.

The church needs to be there at the early symptoms of trouble. Are any of us close enough to the police or the courts that the chief or the judge will say "Here is a boy who needs a man," or "There is a girl who needs a friend?" Are we prepared to be available?

Within our judicial and penal system there is need for professionals who will carry with their vocation a Christian ministry. Perhaps I have read the signs wrong, but I am of the opinion that in days past a Christian who went into social work was suspect. He could have been a doctor or a teacher, a salesman or a plumber. But a Christian social worker was almost a contradiction in terms. I trust we are long past this concept.

Let me plead for more and more of our youth to see a ministry in a vocation of social service. Let me urge that we see such a vocation as not incompatible with an evangelical faith, but rather very compatible to it.

Then there is the need to accept back into society those who have paid their debt. Society finds it hard to forgive. The church—the community of the forgiven—must take the lead in accepting back those who have wasted and lost much of their lives, and whose future will be hard under the best of circumstances.

There are some problems of our society which are distant from some of our congregations. To these problems these congregations find it difficult to respond. I doubt if there is a congregation—large or small, rural or urban—which is not located where youth and adults are running afoul of the law, where the courts and the police would not welcome resources which would reverse the trend—resources which the church has available. Here is an opportunity to merge our social and evangelistic concerns in a redemptive ministry.

The Black Horse
Is on the Way

REVELATION 6:5, 6

For many the "Four Horsemen of the Apocalypse" fit into a prophetic time schedule. Without denying their eschatalogical significance, I select this graphic imagery from the Revelation to remind us all that hunger—The Black Horse—stalks the world, not at some future time, but in the present.

No one is starving (yet) in the areas of Africa to which my recent visit took me. But I was told that last year's crops were short and unless rains come early and in sufficient quantity there will be much hardship. Local newspapers carried accounts of overgrazing and depleted herds. The future does not look hopeful.

My visit to Africa reminded me that most of the peoples of our world live on the border lines of hunger, and for many this line has been crossed. A news release from Bihar, India, which came to my desk this morning describes the need there as "extremely urgent." Recent floods in Pakistan resulted in crops being destroyed. How ironical that too little rain in one area or too much in another has resulted in a shortage of grain and an increase in hunger.

The extended drought in the countries south of the Sahara has taken its toll of crops and grass until the people of the nations of Niger, Chad, Mali, Upper Volta, Mauritanea, and Sengal are on the verge of mass starvation.

Now while this is taking place industrial nations are increasing their demand for and consumption of food. Surpluses once available for areas and times of need are non-existent. The news release from Bihar, earlier referred to, points out that what makes the crisis so grave is that the "government just does not seem to have food available." People cannot eat money. They must have food.

Medical advances and miracle drugs have decreased the mortality rate. The population is increasing at an unprecedented pace. Even if one discounts substantially the forecasts of population prophets, it appears inevitable that a world-wide crisis of hunger is at hand.

To us in United States and Canada this will initially be reflected in higher prices for food and some adjustments in our menus. In much of the world it will be reflected in hollow eyes, listless faces, swollen stomachs, retarded minds, and wasted corpses. (Perhaps this awareness should temper a bit our statements about the high cost of food.)

Christians dare not attempt to escape their responsibility in the face of a crisis of hunger by turning to an eschatalogical fatalism or by the overwhelming size of the task. Compassion calls upon us to do what we can. What can we do?

We can begin by bringing our own standard of living more in line with the realities of the world situation. Most of us will be tempted, and may well be able, to adjust our food budgets in order to maintain our past standard of eating. Is it not a moral issue that the problem for us is that of overeating while many live at a subsistence level? Perhaps it is time to make overeating a spiritual matter as well as a matter of health!

In a congregation I know it was decided to support a meat canning project for the hungry by giving monies saved by means of sacrificial meals rather than using tithe monies. A week was designated for families to save out of the food budget for support for the project.

The idea caught on—especially among the children. The fact of hunger was highlighted at the family level. The funds contributed were beyond expectations—many times the amount traditionally given out of congregational funds. No one suffered nor went very hungry.

This isolated incident illustrates what can be done. Now when this concern becomes more than a special effort but a pattern of life, there will be those who will live instead of die. Both money and food will be saved.

Second, we need to support a Christian ministry of helping people to increase their own food supply. Is this ministry not as necessary, as consistent, and as Christian as the ministry of healing? There are those presently in training whose interest and preparation are to assist people and nations in increasing the productivity of their land in order to feed themselves. "May their tribe increase!"

Is there not something inconsistent about our ministry which emphasizes the saving of life at one stage while making no effort to sustain that life at another critical stage?

Most of us have roots in the good earth. This is said in spite of the fact that many are joining the movement from the farm to the factories and offices. What the farms were to our fathers, the kitchens were to our mothers. These are twin heritages which I believe God and the church could greatly use as we see The Black Horse and rider in the distance. What men can do in increasing productivity, women can support in the area of nutrition. What doctors and nurses do in combating disease, a new ministry can arise in combating hunger and malnutrition.

The parable of Dives and Lazarus is familiar. Often we find the main emphasis of the parable in the irrevocable destiny of Dives rather than in what, according to Jesus, was the cause of that destiny. Selfishness and lack of compassion were the factors, according to the account, which were determinative.

This parable of Dives feasting and Lazarus hoping for the leftovers takes on frightening relevance. If compassion does not move us, how about the prospect of judgment?

The Cost of High Living

For quite some time we have been decrying the high cost of living, while all that time the problem has really been the cost of high living. It's the cost of high living that has finally caught up with us and has brought us to our current crisis.

We seem to be running out of everything. The most apparent and most serious shortage is fuel and energy. The result of this shortage will affect all areas of life. It will result in inconvenience for all and very likely hardship for many.

Although it is easy to be cynical in these days when credibility is at low ebb, I happen to believe that the crisis is a real one. I further believe that until adequate sources of non-fossil energy are found, our lifestyle and the lifestyle of most industrialized nations will be radically affected.

Now this is a two-fold concern of Christians. It is a concern of Christians because of the immediate crisis and the adjustments we need to immediately make to see that essential services continue and suffering and hardship are shared and minimized. The other is longer range and calls us to examine our lifestyle in light of Christ's teaching and the biblical understanding of creation and man's stewardship of it.

Regulations have been imposed upon us which alter our life-style. Christians can and should be above the law (not beyond the law) and impose upon themselves the sacrifices and changes which need to be made. This can be done out of a sense of ought and inner discipline rather than legalism. (One should not have to point out that Christians—regardless of their opinion of the regulation—will obey the laws and regulations which impose rationing, speed limits, needless driving, and thermostat settings). Here is also an opportunity for the church to make a corporate witness to the community. The local congregation may need to look at its program and the use of facilities in light of the present situation. Perhaps the midweek services could meet in homes during the winter months with a savings in heat. If families living in proximity to each other would meet together, there could be a savings in travel. It is possible that we could discover a new fellowship by using the opportunity to invite neighbors to join.

For the corporate worship and Sunday school hour we could ask the members to dress warmly as we turn the thermostat back. We would not be the first generation to worship in unheated or inadequately heated churches. It may be hard to prove that discomfort to the physical increases the experience of the spiritual, but ease and comfort have their own peril, and we have bcome soft and accustomed to comfort. I am reminded of a portion of a poem by Norman Wingert:

> "I like life smooth
> And in the groove
> And all I do be flesh-approved."

Most of us (and this includes Christians) have had too much of everything—too much food, too many clothes, too big cars, too fine homes, and too high thermostats. Purchases have not for most of us been a question of *should*, but primarily of *when*. We eat too much, go too fast, discard too soon. We purchase a riding mower to save our strength and buy exercise machines to gain it back.

Here is an opportunity to discover a new lifestyle that may well be more meaningful, more supportive of those values we know are important, and more biblical. Let visiting, playing games, family projects, and reading replace TV or driving to amusement and recreational locations. Rediscover the pleasure of walking or biking (you will learn to know neighbors whom you have never met). Try gardening instead of more expensive types of recreation. Take a vacation nearer home or even at home (you may have to disconnect the phone). Purchase only what you must have and then only after you have thought about it seriously.

There come events in the life of the church and the experience of Christians that are opportunities to examine our lives in light of our faith and professed Christian commitment. This is just such a time.

It is a good time to examine the warning by Paul of conformity to this world. It is all very well to see in Paul's command a spiritual dimension. It is spiritual in a very profound sense. It is to work from the inside out. But if it is not expressed on the outside—in the living patterns and practices—there is real question if anything very significant has happened on the inside.

This becomes an opportune time to examine our understanding of man's stewardship of God's creation, our concern for our neighbor's welfare, and our tendency toward covetousness. Jesus warned us that life is not made up of the accumulation of things.

The time is opportune for the pulpit to speak God's Word in light of this critical situation. The setting is appropriate for our Bible study groups to examine what God wishes to say to us.

This is not a call to return to caves and candles. It is not a call to homespun clothes and deficient diets. It is not to suggest that we return to horse-drawn vehicles or deny the modern facilities which are an extension of God's creativity.

It is a call to examination, a call to let God's Word and Christ's teaching stand in judgment for our lifestyle. It is a call to nonconformity, sacrifice, stewardship, and Christian concern. It is presented in the conviction that for the Christian the present situation is not a temporary inconvenience but is an opportunity to be light and salt in a society that measures life in terms of possessions, and success in terms of their accumulation.

The Gospel in the Gospels

Regardless of how high may be our doctrine of inspiration, most of us have a canon within the canon. There are Scriptures we turn, to more often. There are others we seldom read. What is true of personal preference is true of preachers, denominations, and traditions. Have you heard any sermons lately from Lamentations, or Judges, or Numbers, or Zephaniah?

There are others we turn to often. Some of us find our message within the eighth century prophets—Amos and Isaiah—as they call for justice and social righteousness, and identify with the least and the lost and the last. Others find the heart of Christian experience in the Acts of the Apostles and seek to pattern their theology and practice after the model of the early church.

There are traditions which find their "canon within the canon" in the Epistles, especially in Galatians, Ephesians, and Romans. I recently read a writer who said that, in his circle, one was suspect as a liberal if he preached from the Gospels rather than from the Epistles. We need to be clear that all things are ours. The Books of the Law, the Writings, the early and the later prophets, the Gospels, the Epistles, the books of beginnings and the books of the last things. They are all a part of God's written revelation.

But God who has spoken through the prophets and by the written word, has now spoken by a Son. The record of this revelation is in the Gospels. It is to the Gospels we must return again and again in order to test our understanding of the Scriptures by the simple, yet profound, teaching of our Lord.

Pentecost is a watershed in the life of the church and in redemption history. It is a crucial event in the understanding of Christian experience. We dare not ignore the role of the Holy Spirit and the Apostles in the revelation of truth. Christ said that this would be one of the functions of the Spirit. In light of this the Acts of the Apostles and the Epistles have great meaning.

What we need to do is to test our understanding of the work of the Holy Spirit and the writings of the Apostles by what the Gospels reveal of him who had the Spirit without measure and who was incarnate truth. We need to pour meaning into Paul's use of the word *faith* by listening to Jesus call men and women to be disciples. Paul's call to nonconformity and separation needs to be understood in terms of him who was in the world but not of it; who was touched but never tainted. John's call to love is nowhere better illuminated than in the Gospel accounts of him who was love incarnate.

The term faith carries varied meanings. Ask a college student for the opposite of faith and he will more than likely say "reason." Ask his parents and they will say "doubt." Ask an evangelical theologian and he will say "works." For the college student faith is accepting what one cannot prove. For the parents faith is belief. For the theologian it is trust or confidence. The Gospels make concrete this call to faith in terms of obedience—following Christ by learning of him and patterning one's life and values after him. If we come to him in repentance and obedience he will save us. This, he said, is the meaning of being a disciple. This is the meaning of faith.

How do we understand the new life in Christ? What is the mark of the regenerate? It is joy and peace and love. It is spiritual fruit and spiritual gifts. It is putting off and putting on. It is caring and sharing. It is denial and dying. We have glimpses of the meaning of these in the Epistles and in the life of the early church. But one turns to the Gospels to see the Christian life clearly and whole, revealed in how he walked.

The church has rediscovered the Holy Spirit. We will better understand the meaning of the Spirit-filled life if, as we read Acts and the Epistles, we also return to the Gospels. The Holy Spirit is Christ-like. He comes in Christ's name. There is One who serves as the plumbline for the testing of the spirits. It is he on whom the Spirit came in fullness. The expression of that fullness in history is found in the Gospels.

The gulf that exists between those who take their direction for justice and righteousness from the prophets, and those who find their direction for an inner experience in the Epistles, is bridged as they meet in the Gospels. He who prayed all night, healed the sick during the day. He who confronted the corruption and hypocrisy of the religious rulers, spoke forgiveness to a repentant sinner. The hand which held the cup and broke the bread, also took a towel and washed the feet.

Neither Corinth nor Jerusalem, Ephesus nor Thessalonica, is the perfect pattern for the nature and mission of the church. The Epistles give direction and correction, but we see in Christ's example what it means to be the body of Christ in the world. We need to test our concept of mission and our outreach in evangelism by his mission and ministry. The temptation to cheap grace and easy discipleship which sometimes comes from misinterpretation of the Epistles finds correction as we hear Jesus call and caution those who would follow.

We do, after all, bear the name of Christ. It would not be amiss to test the image we reflect by the image revealed in the Gospels. This is not a Marcion attempt to deny the Old Testament nor the liberal error to downgrade the Epistles. It is a serious call to rediscover the perspective of the Christ revealed in the Gospels. It is a serious call to test our understanding and our interpretation of the Old Testament and the Epistles by hearing him who was "very God of very God" and "very man of very man."

(Let me give credit to my pastor for watering a seed thought, long dormant. Obviously he should not be held responsible for the specific ideas expressed.)

We're Human, Too

Three faces of man are revealed in the Genesis account—he was created in the image of God, he was created out of the dust of the earth, and he became a sinner in alienation and rebellion against God.

Created in the image of God, he is the highest of God's creation. Indeed, the attainment of man in his dominion over nature is awesome. His creative talent seems to know no limit. His moral sensitivity expressed in conscience is a residue of his divine image. When made a new creation by God's grace, his life brings a ray of divine light into a darkened world and the image of God is more truly reflected.

But all too evident is his sinful state in which the image of God has been marred and perverted. In fact, it is his glory that has made his shame the more shameful. Refusing to live in his subordinate state in obedience to God, he sought to be as God, and in this rebellious act lost his fellowship with God and alienated himself from his fellowmen. Pride separated him from God and selfishness alienated him from his brothers. The pages of history are filled with the record of his fallenness.

The third characteristic of his nature is his creaturehood. This is graphically portrayed when the accounts relate that man was formed of the dust of the ground. In the 103rd Psalm the Psalmist writes of man as dust and as the flower of the field and like grass.

These terms do not speak of man's lack of value but they do speak of his creaturehood—his identification with creation and the transitory nature of his earthly existence. As creature, man is finite and limited. He is subject to the perils of creaturehood. He becomes hungry and needs food. He becomes tired and needs rest. He becomes ill and needs healing; he dies and returns to dust. All that which is part of his physical nature—mind, body, and emotions—is subject to the wear and tear of existence.

Our creaturehood—our humanity—in no way makes us worthless before God. However limited may be our human endowments, we are loved by God even as sinners, and when we come to him he becomes our Father. Indeed, the tone of Scripture seems to be that God is especially on the side of the poor and the helpless—those who may be the least endowed with creaturely assets.

The effectiveness of our Christian life will be determined by how we accept the limitation of our creaturely existence. As creatures we are born to all of the contingencies of creaturehood. This lesson we need to learn. God's grace does not alter this fact. No matter the degree of spiritual attainment, we are limited in our judgment, finite in our wisdom, and transitory in our existence.

God gives us grace to live with this fact. He supplies our daily needs. He gives direction and wisdom and strength for the tasks of life. But in none of these do we escape the bonds of earth or the destiny of dust.

We would understand more about the problems of "unanswered" prayer if we would take seriously this fact of our nature. How many of our prayers, which seem to us to be unanswered, are really prayers to escape our creaturehood?

This is particularly pertinent when we pray for healing for ourselves or others. Too often the failure to realize an answer to a prayer for healing is attributed to a lack of faith or to some reason beyond us of why God does not heal. A third element may need to be considered and that is the fact of our creaturehood.

"Man that is born of a woman is of few days, and full of trouble. He cometh forth like a flower and is cut down . . ." (Job 14:1, 2).

There is another element of man's creaturehood that impinges upon our spiritual experience. The Christian life is concerned with behavior and relationships and attitudes. Obviously these are related to the spiritual life. Selfishness, pride, jealousy, and covetousness are sins condemned in Scripture which result in attitudes and relationships and behavior that are also sinful.

But there are also patterns of behavior and attitudes and relationships which are rooted, not in our sinful nature, but in our humanity. Some of us are quick and decisive. Others are slow and tedious. Some are reflective, others are activists. Some are expressive; others are reserved. Some are quick of temper; others are passive. One could go on and on.

Now in a community of faith such as the congregation, these human characteristics need to be taken into account as well as those manifestations of our sinful nature. Interpersonal relations can be hindered because persons of diverse personalities find it difficult to work together. Attitudes that seem to reflect carnal opposition may be simply a natural reluctance to change or innovation.

This is more than just an observation on interpersonal relations. The recognition of these two elements in all of our lives and in a congregational setting is important if we are to recognize the real enemy and distinguish between sin and humanity.

It should be the concern of the pastor and of each of us as members to recognize the difference between that which arises out of the fallenness of our nature and that which is a legitimate expression of our creaturehood. The former should be dealt with in confession and repentance, surrender and cleansing. These are the works of the flesh and are to be put off. One of the disciplines of our Christian lives is to analyze our behavior, reactions, relationships, and attitudes to determine if their origin may, in fact, be in our fallenness.

But there remains those characteristics which are normal and human. How do we live with them? The grace of God is available here as well.

I should like to believe that God's love and grace in my life would compensate to a degree for those less desirable qualities in my character and personality—qualities which are a part of my humanness. Even some of the rough edges may be smoothed out. Hopefully, I would be conscious of my less desirable traits and attempt to refine them. I could hope that the same would happen to those with whom I fellowship in the body of Christ. So we have not only become *new* people but are becoming *nice* people in our pilgrimage together.

But I confess that I have more hope in God's grace dealing with this in another way. That he will give me a love that will see beyond those characteristics in my brother or sister that run across the grain of my life. And that, similarly, grace will be given to my brother or sister to love and appreciate me in spite of those things in my life that run counter to the grain in theirs.

This is not "enduring" grace. This is loving grace. This is not a matter of "putting up" with my brother or sister, but of accepting one another as human with all that that means, and at the same time enjoying each other as children of God and brothers and sisters in Christ.

The Battle
and the Skirmishes

Within the past year I sat in a meeting where a rather well-known evangelist amazed an audience of editors with graphic accounts and lurid details of demon possession and demonic manifestation. The interest (one could almost call it fascination) with the occult and the demonic is high on the interest scale of both Christian and non-Christian.

We take a prurient interest in the bizarre. The more lurid the details, the more abnormal the manifestations, the more evil is the incident.

Now one of the values of this new interest in the demonic is a recognition of the reality of evil. Evil is more than ignorance or man's humanity and finiteness. Man's problems are deeper than the social influences and the combination of genes. There is a reality to evil which affects the destiny of men and with which we must reckon.

The danger is that we will become so fascinated with the bizarre manifestations that we will miss the more crucial evidences of evil.

The temptations Jesus faced in the wilderness were not as dramatic manifestations of demonic power as the mad man of Gadara, but they were just as real and, let me say, more crucial. The seeking of position, the love of money, the escape from cross bearing, the acceptance of worldly values, the worship of Caesar, and the critical spirit are more devastating to the cause of Christ than the reported orgies of demon worship.

Whatever realities these strange manifestations may have, they may well be diversionary tactics of the enemy. By these Satan takes our attention from where the real battles are being fought and we concentrate on the skirmishes. There may be a lot of gore and smoke but the real issues of life are being settled—won or lost—on a broader front.

Let's not become intrigued by the traditional image, and at present the contemporary image, of a lecherous, beady-eyed, sub or super-human personage whose presence brings with it sulphuric odors. More than likely the devil really wears a Hart, Schaffner, and Marx suit. He smells freshly groomed and his shoes are well polished. His mien is sophisticated and gracious. He will offer you the kingdom of this world—at least a part of it. He promises position and honor. He suggests a way to escape the cross as in Peter's suggestion to Christ (you recall Christ's reply). He comes in the temptation to deny Christ and disobey him. All the while we do not even recognize him.

So while we divert our attention to the skirmishes the enemy has encircled us. And we do not even know it.

God's Accounting Method

Our most subtle temptations are in the area of the legitimate and the necessary.

For the Christian, materialism is a more likely temptation than demonism, gluttony more common than drunkenness, and immorality a greater peril than gambling.

The reason is that all of these—gluttony, materialism, and immorality—are related to essential and proper functions. We can do without alcohol, but eating is essential to life. Sexuality is essential to the survival of the race and is a God-given drive. Our material world is an expression of God's creative act. It is necessary for our existence. God called it good. Man was given lordship over it, and the temptation to call it our own is very real.

Herein lies the peril. The temptation to misuse the good is more subtle than the temptation to yield to evil. The desert temptations of Jesus reflect this to a degree—turning stones to bread, casting himself upon God's saving power, and bringing to himself all the nations of the world. The Bible recognizes this fact and warns Christians repeatedly about the peril. In no area is this more true than in relation to possessions and money.

As Christians we are to accept God's creation with thanksgiving and reverence. It may sound trite and overly pious, but it is nevertheless true: we have nothing except what has been given. Neither our lives nor our possessions are really our own. They belong to God. We are stewards of our gifts and of his creation.

This is why Jesus and the apostles had as much to say about money and possessions as they did. They warned against the peril of riches, the sin of covetousness, and the love of money. The love of money was the root of all evil. Covetousness was as idolatry. The camel could go through the needle's eye easier than a rich man could enter heaven.

Jesus does give us some help in our attitude towards our possessions. He said that it was possible to convert them into eternal securities. This not only preserved their value—beyond the reach of moths and rust and thieves—it also had an effect on the destiny of one's heart. The heart follows the treasure.

When we invest that treasure, God does a unique kind of accounting. The value of our investment is determined by the amount we have left. As the proverbial two-edged sword, God's method of accounting cuts both ways. It is both comforting and disquieting.

Inflation and Morality

The causes of inflation are complex but the underlying problems are moral and spiritual.

Since the causes of inflation are basically moral, they are not as responsive to the economic policies of the state as is recession.

Stated very simply, inflation is an over-supply of money to purchase a limited supply of goods and services. To that degree the problem appears economic. The causes, however, are moral.

When business takes undue profits or condones inefficient or monopolistic practices, the cost of an item exceeds its value. When that item (goods or service) is a necessity which people must purchase, the inflationary tendency is inevitable.

When labor's productivity does not keep pace with labor's wages, the result is purchasing power growing faster than the supply of goods and services—the ability to purchase exceeds the ability to supply, and prices rise as consumers compete for the limited supply.

When the consumer spends not only what he has but that which he hopes to have, the supply of money (credit) exceeds productivity. This is because the consumer has only produced to the date of his purchase but has purchased in terms of his earnings eight or nine weeks or more in the future.

When governments live on credit (deficits) it has the same effect as credit in the private sector—only more so.

When efforts are expended and wages paid for services and goods which do not satisfy human needs and consumer demands, purchasing power is not matched by an equal supply of goods and services. The scarce commodities are bid up in an inflationary spiral. The ninety-billion dollar defense budget in the United States is an example of gross imbalance of productivity and purchasing power. When men are paid to destroy rather than produce, the inflationary results are obvious.

The moral factor in all of this economic jargon is simply this: when business profits are excessive, when labor does not give sixty minutes of labor for an hour of pay, when consumers and governments are unwilling to live within their means, and when huge sums and productive potential are spent for destruction rather than the meeting of human needs, we are dealing with moral issues.

The Bible is not a textbook on economics, but it is a book on morality and stewardship. In fact the Bible speaks quite specifically to most, if not all, of the aspects of the problem we have briefly stated.

Inflation is a moral issue just as thievery is a moral issue.

To our Bibles, we who are Christians. Hear the words of Isaiah, the teachings of Jesus, and the writings of Paul and James. Most of us will be amazed to learn what they say about the subject.

Mobility and Congregational Growth

We say it on Youth Sunday and at other times when the emphasis is upon youth. It has become almost a *cliche.*

"Youth are the church of tomorrow."

That statement is misleading on two counts.

Youth are not the church of the future. Youth are the church of the present. To assume that our young people are to be seen and not heard is to deprive a congregation of the contribution which youth can uniquely make.

Many congregations have found that their youth have brought an openness, an honesty, and a commitment that results in new life to the group. The prophecy of Joel is for many congregations taking on new meaning for it is the young—our own sons and daughters—that are sensitive to the Spirit.

The statement is also misleading when we see in the youth of the congregation the future of that congregation. The mobility of our population is against us. In most cases the youth of the congregation will not continue to live in that community nor worship, upon reaching adulthood, in the congregation in which they grew up.

The reality of this fact of our society will vary from congregation to congregation. But it would be an interesting study for a congregation to determine the number of "second generation" adult members. That is, how many of the present resident members, over twenty-one years of age, were born to families of the congregation.

A second survey that would be enlightening would be to try to determine what has happened to those who were children of the congregation. Go back to the 50's and list those who were children and youth (5-21) during that time and determine where they are, their relation to the denomination or to another church, and the degree of commitment.

This kind of exercise will, in most cases, have two effects.

Congregations will realize that what they and the home are going to do in influencing and nurturing their youth will need to be done by the late teens. When the youth leave for college or trade schools or employment, the opportunity which the local congregation has is about finished. This should call for serious evaluation of the youth ministry of a local church and the need to encourage commitment prior to the severance of congregational-residential ties.

Even though commitment for some may not be as clear and as definite as we may desire, the teaching will not be lost. What is even more lasting is the memory of the life and lives in the congregation in which they grew up—or at least in which they spent their impressionable and discerning years. If those memories are of a caring and loving and committed fellowship, where creed was reflected in life, the chances for identification with a congregation in their new place of residence are good.

The other effect which a survey will have will be the awareness that congregations depending upon holding the children of families for their numerical growth will slowly die. Congregational growth in our mobile society must occur in the reaching of community families. Some of these families will be new families in the community. Mobility does not only mean loss, it also means opportunity. People who move *from* also move *to*.

A Word Lightly Used

It was not the faith of the three Hebrew children that brought them out of that fiery furnace. It was their faith that took them in.

We have a tendency to identify faith with the miraculous and see a direct relationship between the degree of faith and the manifestation of the miraculous. A reading of Hebrews 11 should give us a more biblical perspective. Whether they "escaped the edge of the sword" (v. 34) or were "killed with the sword" (v. 37) did not alter the fact of their faith. Faith was evidenced by their faithfulness to God's call.

Faith is not essentially an attitude of the mind or emotions, but an act of the will. It is the conversion of belief into act and trust into obedience. Abraham's faith was evidenced in his faithfulness to God's call. When he heard God's call in Ur, he said to Sara, "Let's start packing!" They moved to Haran. Some years later he heard God's call again. He said to Sara, "Did you save the boxes? It's again time to pack. We are moving to Canaan." Then there was the night when he heard God speak that incredible word: "Take your son, your only son Isaac . . ." He rose early. This time he did the packing and began that long journey to Mount Moriah.

We today use the word so lightly. It is part of our conversion formula. Sometimes it is used as synonymous with belief. Other times it is little more than presumption. Sometimes it is identified with our using God for our purposes.

We would do well to restore to *faith* its biblical meaning of faithfulness and obedience. Supportive of this effort is to recall that it was faith that took the three Hebrew children into the furnace. It was God that brought them out.

The Christian and Vocation

There are Christians who depreciate their secular vocation. When asked what their vocation is they will answer somewhat like this: "My vocation is teaching a class of boys in our Sunday school. I keep books for a living."

This response may have numerous variations. The common element is that the day-to-day vocation is not where the action really is. The real part of living does not take place until the buzzer sounds and it ceases in the morning when the time card is punched.

When this is the case it means that we spend the major part of our waking hours in a task that lacks real meaning. We identify our vocation as "making a living."

Without question there have been and will be those who sense a call to a ministry which has no means of financial support. Giving one's self to such a ministry means that a minimum income must be found to meet one's needs. This income from a secular vocation may be the sole purpose of the task.

But what are legitimate exceptions should not invalidate the principle that Christians should consider their vocations as avenues of service to God and their fellow men and that the pay check is not a sufficient reason for a vocation.

As suggested earlier, there will be those who by choice will find the real meaning of life, not in their five-day-week job, but in those after-hours and weekend ministries.

There will be others who, because of circumstances and limitation, will find themselves in jobs that are honorable but hardly satisfying. For them, meaning and satisfaction will be found in family or church or witnessing or service.

Family and church, witnessing and service are surely worthy of our time and efforts. But life will be more biblical if we see our work as a ministry and a service to God and man. There is a measure of common sense in choosing a vocation that is meaningful.

My concern is for those who have the opportunity to make such choices. List in your mind or on paper the obvious needs in our world—food, health care, penal reform, justice, good literature, energy—the list is long. Then list vocations which contribute to meeting these needs.

World hunger will not be solved by our charity or sacrifice, as important as both of these have been. What is needed are men and women who will choose a vocation in agriculture and foods, and work with all nations in the production of food and in its consumption. Penal reform will not really be solved by those who visit prisoners on weekends, as commendable as that ministry is. Justice and reform within our penal system will occur when Christians choose those vocations which bear directly on this area of our nation's life. Men and women who bring their skills and devotion to bear upon the structures of our society that control the system.

What we are calling for is the awareness that secular vocations are God's calling and a part of this work just as are the spiritual vocations of pastor and missionary.

One of the results of this concept of vocation would be the releasing of those called to a spiritual ministry for that ministry. There are knowledgeable persons who claim that the mission outreach of the church becomes sidetracked by the church's involvement in education, health care, and other material and social ministries. The good news became lost in good works. I have more trouble separating these two than some have. But it is very likely that those prepared, gifted, called, and sent to proclaim by word the Good News have found themselves so involved in a ministry of Good Works, with the accompanying administrative duties, that the proclamation was neglected and the Good News almost inaudible.

My plea is that the secular vocations support the religious vocations in the church's ministry, and that they both be seen as Christian ministries. It may well call for the same financial sacrifice and change in lifestyle. But what it will do is to bring in a direct manner our secular vocation into the realm of Christian service. The Christian witness will not be what it should be if it is carried on only by those in religious and spiritual vocations and in the spare time of the 90% of Christians who chose secular ones.

Our secular vocations must come under the lordship of Christ, the pattern of servanthood, and to use an old but biblical term "placed upon the altar."

On Loving One's Neighbor

Northern Indiana is in the midst of the corn harvest. Corn harvesters, slowly moving through the fields, dot the countryside. Traffic slows as a tractor pulling a load of yellow grain moves toward the elevator. Day and night the noise of our neighbor's drier indicates that he is holding his grain for feeding or a higher price.

What is happening here is being repeated again and again across the country. This marks the closing weeks of a harvest of wheat and barley, beans and corn that began early in the summer and moved northward into the provinces of Canada and the corn belt of the United States.

In the midst of such bounty it is difficult to think seriously of words such as hunger, malnutrition, starvation, and famine. But these words will not go away. Although at present they do not make headlines, they are a constant threat or reality to hundreds of millions in our world. Countries with food problems will fall far short of meeting their people's needs.

What is the Christian response to the fact of food shortage and the specter of hunger and famine?

1. **The Christian should examine his or her lifestyle and stewardship in light of the neighbor's need.** Can Christians afford to go "first class" when their brothers and neighbors cannot go at all? An examined lifestyle will reflect itself in our accountability for goods and monies in a ministry to the world's needy.

The Christian's response is not based upon the hope of society's redemption as expressed by the "social gospel," but rather on the command of Jesus to love one's neighbor as he loves himself.

2. **The Christian should be aware that man does not live by bread alone.** This quotation by Jesus asserts two truths. Man needs bread. Bread alone is not enough. To deny man's need of bread by one's theology or practice is to deny the plain teaching of Scripture. Men need bread. This is the way God created us.

But bread is not enough. Man need the words of God. One needs to tread carefully in relating Christianization and economic well-being. But when non-Christian practices and superstitious beliefs militate against obedience to God and his laws and the stewardship of resources, the acceptance of the gospel is an asset in the struggle for survival.

Let it be said again that economic well-being is not the certain result of, nor the principal motive for, evangelism. But when the problems of a people have their roots in religion, the solution to those problems may well be found in the Christian gospel.

3. **Christian vocation should be chosen in light of the problem of hunger.** Charity is a needed and worthy expression of Christian love. But charity will not solve the problem of world hunger. More and more Christians need to wrestle with vocational decisions in the light of need rather than in terms of remuneration.

As serious a problem as is hunger, this is a problem that has the possibility of solution. There are ways to deal with population growth that are morally and ethically acceptable to the Christian. The potential of increased food production is not yet taxed. We have the means of bringing the population line and the food line on the graph together.

We need men and women who will take the vocations related to food and nutrition and agriculture as seriously as their fathers and mothers took teaching and medicine and nursing care.

4. **Christians—especially in Canada and the United States—can appeal to their governments to place their resources in the battle against hunger and malnutrition.**

We have written letters before to our government regarding the right to read the Bible from outer space and for the right to pray in the classroom. We have written for freedom on the air waves on behalf of gospel broadcasts. We have written in an effort to clean up the newsstands and television.

Now put yourself in the place of a father unable to find any food for his hungry family who meet him hollow-eyed and listless as he returns to his village. Or see yourself as a mother holding a child too weak to cry and growing thinner each day. Then remember the words of the Scriptures which call for us to love our neighbor as we love ourselves. Then write a letter.

The Four-fold Witness

I CORINTHIANS 15:3-8

The word *witness* is a term lightly used and often misunderstood. Its interpretation is sometimes so broad as to include the role of the prosecutor and the judge. Other times it is limited to personal experience, confined to what has happened to the one bearing witness.

In the early verses of Paul's great discourse on the resurrection in I Corinthians 15, he identifies four characteristics of the Christian witness which add wholeness to it.

The Christian witness is historical. The Christian faith is rooted in history. It is concerned with One who lived in a certain time and place. It is concerned with events that really happened. The Christian faith is anchored in the death, burial, and resurrection of Jesus Christ.

When the apostles fulfilled their role as witnesses, it was their witness to the resurrection. This Jesus whom the mob had demanded to be crucified God had raised up. Everything was different since that event. These men and women now needed to take a new look at life and their attitudes.

When the foundations are shaken and questions exceed the answers, and the spiritual glow of yesterday has passed in the night, it is time to return to the empty tomb and from there begin to put things back together again.

The Christian witness is theological. Now, do not let that word frighten you. It means that the historical event has spiritual meaning. "Christ died for our sins . . . and was raised in accordance with the Scriptures." Theology is the biblical meaning of a biblical event or truth, in this case the cross and the resurrection.

The theological part of the Christian witness understands and explains man's need and God's provision. Man's malady is seen in the light of the cross. God's provision is seen in the cross and the empty tomb. It is the obligation of the church to plumb the depths of the meaning of sin and grace, of the cross and the resurrection. The source of this meaning is the Scriptures. Our witness needs to include not only the knowledge of the Scriptures, but their meaning as well.

The Christian witness is experiential. It is born out in the lives of people who commit themselves to the Risen Christ. Christ—the Resurrected Christ—was seen of Peter, the twelve, five hundred, and James. The historical fact and the biblical meaning were supported by personal encounter.

Christ appeared to Peter—boastful, profane, weak, and repentant. He appeared to the twelve—confused and fearful. He walked with two on an afternoon on the road to Emmaus—two who had lost hope.

This Christ still meets men and women in their need. He speaks forgiveness and implants hope. He brings new life and frees the prisoner. The church of Jesus Christ is part of the Christian witness. The historical fact and the biblical meaning are confirmed in an innumerable host of men and women who have met the Resurrected Christ.

The Christian witness is also personal. Paul writes ". . . he appeared also to me." This was no second-hand faith for Paul. He too had met the Christ. The encounter on the Damascus road made the difference. The rumor of the resurrection was now a fact of history, confirmed in his own experience.

It continues to be true—the motivation to witness and the credibility of that witness comes from a first-hand faith. It is important to remember that this personal encounter is with the same Christ who appeared to Peter and Paul and the twelve. It is the same Christ who has met Christians during these intervening centuries. It is personal, yet within the Christian tradition. It is different, yet the same.

We restrict and hinder our witness if we neglect one or more of these aspects of the Christian witness. Our witness needs to be anchored in history, interpreted by Scripture, confirmed in experience, and made credible by a personal encounter with this Christ of history and the Bible.

Realism and Tradition

When we observe Mother's Day and Father's Day, Children's Day and Family Week in the traditional manner, we have very clearly ignored a sizeable segment of our society and of our church membership. It is easy to make assumptions in this area of ministry that will not stand up under scrutiny.

One household in five consists of a single person. One household in three consists of two persons. Nearly 35 million households consist of one or two persons only.

These statistics reflect a number of influences at work in our society—the effects of divorce, the death of a mate, the postponement of children, the increased recognition of the integrity of singleness, the mobility of society resulting in grown children living at great distance from parents, and increased longevity. These are conditions existing in any congregation that reflects to any degree the community of which it is a part.

Whatever the reason, this is a fact with which the church must reckon. If we continue to write and teach and preach as though every person was a member of the traditional family—two parents with three or four children still in the home—we will have ignored a high percentage of our audience.

This is not a call to remain silent in our ministry to the family— parents and child—but it is a reminder that the needs of our members are diverse. If we are to minister to our communities, the church will increasingly reflect the diversity of our society.

The recognition of this diversity needs to be a congregational concern in the total life of the church. It needs to be recognized beyond the appropriate preaching and teaching ministries. Acceptance is needed within the congregation for each other— regardless of marital or family status.

To a great extent the extended family of a past generation— several generations living in a geographical proximity and in a familial relationship—needs to be replaced by the community of faith—the family of God—gathered in life and worship.

I know of a situation where the family is removed by distance from other members of their extended family—grandparents, uncles, and aunts. When the parents were preparing their will, the concern for guardianship of the children was faced. The parents, I understand, seriously considered naming the congregation, with which they worshiped and of which they were a part, as the guardian of their children.

The legality of such a proposal was not tested. My friends took the traditional approach. But the idea should not be ignored as unrealistic and novel. Should not the congregation become the new extended family for the members, the diversity within the congregation contributing to the wholeness of families and individuals?

This calls for more than appropriate preaching and teaching and interest-based activities. This could well be an expression of what Jesus meant when he spoke of those who did his will as his brothers and sisters, fathers and mothers.

The Sin of Covetousness

I had always interpreted the commandment against covetousness with the emphasis upon "thy neighbor's" phrase. The sinful aspect was in desiring that which belonged to someone else. King Ahab was for me the classic example in his desire for a vineyard that belonged to Naboth.

Then I decided to preach a sermon on covetousness and attempted to discover what Jesus meant when, to the group gathered around him, he said "... beware of covetousness ..." (Luke 12:15) and what Paul meant when he said, "Mortify therefore ... covetousness, which is idolatry" (Colossians 3:5). To my amazement (and discomfort) I found that the meaning of *pleonexia* was not related to wanting that which was already the possession of another but referred to "wanting more."

"Beware," Jesus said, "of wanting more, for life does not consist in the accumulation of things." "Put to death," writes Paul, "that desire for more, for it is like the sin of idolatry." In the Colossian verse the practices listed along with covetousness are a sordid lot. But it is for covetousness alone that the label of idolatry is reserved.

Idolatry was the sin of sins among the nations of Israel. This distinction was reserved for idolatry because it reflected more than disobedience. It was, in fact, the transfer of affection. It is this characteristic of covetousness which is so perilous to the Christian.

In recent years two of the reportedly world's wealthiest men died. If the media's reports of these men's lives is substantially accurate, they are modern day examples of the truth of Jesus' words that, "a man's life consisteth not in the abundance of the things which he possesseth."

Over against this somewhat negative approach to the material world are the complementary biblical teachings of God's ownership and our stewardship, and Jesus' clear teaching on love for neighbor and the servant posture for the Christian.

As radical as it may sound in our consumer-oriented society, the. warning is clear, distinct, and biblical:

Beware of wanting more. It is the modern idolatry.

A Look at Gifts

The word *charismatic* has become a well-used term in the current religious scene. The word is a transliteration of the Greek word *charisma* which means *gift* and comes from the root *charis* which is translated *grace* or *favor*. A charismatic in the current use of the term is one who has received a gift of ministry in keeping with Romans 12 and I Corinthians 12.

The significance of the word is that an ability to minister has been received from God. These gifts, listed in the Roman and Corinthian passages, include prophecy, service, teaching, exhortation, miracles, healing, helpers, administration, and speaking in various kinds of tongues.

There is a tendency to confine the meaning of charismatic to the "speaking in various kinds of tongues." The speaking in tongues is not mentioned at all in Romans 12 while in I Corinthians 12 it is listed as one of a number of gifts. The word for the speaking in tongues is *glossolalia*. We get our word *glossary* from the root *glossa*. It is inaccurate and unbiblical to limit our understanding or focus our emphasis of the charismatic to the speaking in tongues or to make the two synonymous.

The charismatic movement requires all of us to examine our understanding of the gifts of the Spirit. There are two common approaches to this scriptural concept. There is the approach that contrasts the gifts of the Spirit with the fruit of the Spirit and emphasizes the fruit to the neglect of the gift. There are good grounds for highlighting the fruit of the Spirit. Paul's interjection of the Hymn to Love (I Corinthians 13)—in the midst of his treatment of gifts as "a still more excellent way" is significant. Jesus' own statement in Matthew 7:21-23 suggests that obedience to the Word is more important than the ability to work miracles and do mighty works. But by this approach we have a tendency to detour around the teaching on gifts.

The other approach is to equate gifts with natural abilities and to see the ability to speak fluently or reason logically as gifts of the Spirit for use in the church. This approach admits that miraculous gifts may have been evident in the New Testament church but are no longer the source of church ministries.

This later interpretation needs to be examined for us to be certain that we understand the biblical meaning of gifts of the Spirit. As the church moves in faith and reaches those not nurtured in the Christian faith, I believe that we will surely need those whose ministry can only be explained as a gift by the Spirit to the church. It is likely that God will equip a growing church by giving gifts to those who are being saved rather than by selecting those for salvation who have special abilities. An understanding of the biblical teaching on gifts is closely related to church growth.

When we stop to discuss spiritual gifts, the question of tongues is never far away. In fact, as stated earlier, the speaking in tongues appears many times to dominate the subject of spiritual gifts. We wish to make several brief observations regarding the current emphasis upon the speaking "in various kinds of tongues."

First: We need to come to terms with the apparent difference between Pentecostal tongues (Acts 2:4-8) and Corinthian tongues (I Corinthians 14). The "other tongues" on Pentecost were for communication. Those visitors at Jerusalem heard "the mighty works of God" in their own language. Corinthian tongues are not intelligible unless interpreted. While the one aids communication, the other delays; the one is understood by the hearers, the other is hidden from the hearer.

Both the character and the purpose of Corinthian tongues are in contrast to the Pentecost experience.

Second: The thrust of I Corinthians 12 and 14 is to de-emphasize tongues and to emphasize prophecy (to proclaim God's Word). At the beginning of the chapter (I Corinthians 14:1-5) and at the close, Paul *permits* tongues but *promotes* prophecy. In the final verses of chapter 12 Paul appears to give a value structure to the gifts. Following apostles at the head of the list is prophecy, and the last gift on the list is tongues.

We may well reflect on the fact that in the other two Scriptures (Romans 12 and Ephesians 4) where gifts are referred to, no mention is made of tongues. In fact the Corinthian letter is the only reference to tongues in the Epistles.

Third: It is apparent that everyone does not receive all the gifts. The answer to Paul's rhetorical questions at the close of I Corinthians 12 is "No!" Not everyone is an apostle nor a prophet nor a speaker in tongues. It is God "who apportions to each one individually as he wills" (I Corinthians 12:11). It is certainly inappropriate to test a person's spiritual standing or the validity of his experience on the basis of the presence or the absence of a particular gift, or of any gift, for that matter.

Fourth: We need to recognize the God-given faculty of reason. One of the casualties resulting from the charismatic movement has been reason and reasonable judgment. Paul in I Corinthians 14:13-16 highlights the need to bring the power of the mind upon our spiritual life and expression. "For if I pray in a tongue, my spirit prays but my mind is unfruitful." In verse 19 he states that five words with the mind are of more value in church "than 10,000 words in a tongue."

This negation of man's reason and rational judgment is one of the frightening aspects of the charismatic movement. The denial of reason is particularly evident in the ecstatic experience of tongues. Reason is surely a mark of God's image in man and we negate this at our spiritual peril.

In all of this Paul calls upon the Corinthian church to exercise love. One of the characteristics of love is the respect each has for the other. This Paul saw as essential in the midst of the charismatic manifestations at Corinth.

The need is no less today. Our experience should constantly be subject to the Scriptures. Until we come to the unity of the faith we need to exercise love and understanding—not judging one another on the basis of the presence or the absence of gifts. Rather we thank God for each other and accept each other as members of the Body of Christ, being grateful for our diversity which completes the body and enables it to function.

Keeping the Fire Tended

My earlier years were lived in settings where a wood or coal burning heater was our source of heat. These heaters had certain advantages—on a cold night they contributed greatly to family togetherness in a way that central heating does not and fireplaces seek to recapture.

But these heaters had disadvantages. They were not automatic. One needed to occasionally shake the grate, often stir the fire, and constantly add wood or coal.

Early in my life I acquired a love for reading. If my parents were away for the evening I could happily spend a winter's evening seated, with my book, near the heater. It was not uncommon for my parents, upon their return, to find me very close to the heater with the fire almost burned out.

Absorbed by the contents of the book I would forget to care for the fire. As the fire burnt lower I would move closer, until I was almost against the stove which no longer was providing much heat.

My experience with that hand-fed heater is a parable of our

Christian lives. We need to keep the fire tended. Else, it will burn low and indeed go out. It follows, that on occasion we need to check the fire.

Engrossed in our secular duties and religious activities, pressured by the world and our own desires, we neglect the tending of the inner life. We are unaware that we have grown cold. We need to feed the fire, stir the embers, and at times shake the grate.

Recently I was introduced to John Wesley's order of worship for an examination service. This he had prepared to be observed by his classmeetings. The service of examination and dedication and worship was in the Anglican (Church of England) tradition. I suspect the liturgy would need some modification to be meaningful to us. I refer to it here because of its timing, its purpose, and its method.

Wesley's concern for the holy life did not disappear with Aldersgate. He found an inner source unknown before, but the disciplines necessary were to be cultivated. These disciplines he sought to instill in the converts to Methodism. The service of examination and worship was one of these occasions.

One of the parts of that service which I found of interest was John Wesley's emphasis upon confession. Confession of sin was a part of the ritual. I found this of interest because I did not associate this ritual with Wesley's theology. Certainly, I was prepared for repentance and confession to be the necessary response to an awareness of sin. What I was not prepared for was the inclusion of this in a corporate ritual to be made a deliberate part of a planned service.

It is not my purpose to begin a dialogue on Wesleyan theology but rather to point out Wesley's assumption that we need to take care of our spiritual fires consciously and deliberately. "Examine yourselves, to see whether you are holding to your faith" (II Corinthians 13:5). If such an examination reveals sin, confession is the order of the day. Let us not allow our theology to stand in the way of our need for confession and repentance.

Now back to tending the fire.

Our spiritual life needs to be constantly nurtured and fed. The disciplines of worship, fellowship, Bible study, prayer, and Christian reading are essential elements in keeping the fires burning. It is difficult to maintain a warm, glowing spiritual life if any one of these elements is neglected.

In the pressures of our schedules it is easy for these disciplines to be neglected. No dramatic event results from this neglect, just the slow dying of the fire, with joy and peace and love among the casualties.

Occasionally we must stir the fire to renew its vigor and life. Just such occasions need to be part of the Christian discipline. We can easily equate activity with spiritual life. If we are busy in the life of the church—teaching, sewing, singing, administering—we surely must be devoted Christians. Obviously, there is a correlation between spiritual life and service, but they are not the same. It is possible for activity to be a substitute for devotion and a means of drowning the cry of the heart.

There is the need to examine our motives and our devotion, our priorities and our loyalties. What is it that we really love? Is ours the single eye and the undivided heart. The Danish theologian, Soren Kierkegaard, stated that "purity of heart is to will one thing." Jesus said that we are to love God with all our heart, soul, mind and strength and to seek first the kingdom of God.

The peril for the Christian lies not so much in the forbidden areas of life—although when the fire dies down these become real perils—but rather in the necessary and legitimate elements of life. Those things which are needful tend to come before the kingdom. We seek first "all these other things" and hope to have the kingdom of Heaven added.

The warmth and life of our spiritual fire will be governed by our relationships with others. Are there those you would just as soon not meet? Are you carrying around an unkind attitude towards another person? Is there need to straighten out a relationship—apologize or confess? It is clear from Scripture that there is a direct and inescapable relationship between our relationship to others and our relationship with God. Jesus said, "First be reconciled to your brother, and then come and offer your gift" (Matthew 5:24).

We must maintain the disciplines of Christian devotion, examine the priorities and loyalties by which we really govern our lives, look carefully at our relations with others—family, congregation, neighbors, and fellow-employees, and despise not confession of sin when we find it.

He that does these things will keep the fire burning.

"Grandpa's Money
Will Never Get All"

The experience of cold winter weather reminds us all of man's vital dependence upon nature and nature's resources. Whether it is water for irrigation, or rain for the vast wheat and corn fields, or fuel to heat our homes and power our industries, man is helpless in the face of nature's deviation from the norm to which we have geared our lifestyle and designed our economies.

This should foster a sense of humility. Man is not the master of his fate. His accomplishments are many and awesome, but his dependence and vulnerability must be recognized. I find it important to remind myself and my family that the food on our table is there by the providence of God. In recent weeks we have reminded ourselves that the gas in the furnace is also there as a result of his providence.

A few inches short in annual rainfall, a few degrees' variation in the temperature, a few seconds of shifting in the fault lines, and we are aware that not only we, but indeed our civilization, are subject to the providence and mercy of God. This is a humbling experience.

Experiences such as this should as well remind us of our prodigality. My mother used to tell the story of a family who inherited a sizeable fortune from their grandfather. Cautioned about their free-spending lifestyle, their response, according to the account, was to wave a handful of paper money and say, "Grandpa's money will never get all."

Their logic was as poor as their grammar. The point of my mother's story was that it did "get all." We are not unlike the characters of the story. We live as though it will never "get all." Whether it is oil, gas, coal, land, water, minerals, or air, our concern is immediate rather than future. Eat, drink, and be merry for it will never "get all"!

We trust in the unlimited supply of our natural resources and in man's ingenuity. We live as if there was no tomorrow. We could well ask what is the legacy we are leaving to our children and theirs. We do not do much to alter this prodigality when we only look at others whose lifestyle we envy but cannot afford. Living responsibly is a question with which each of us must come to terms.

If anyone is tempted to see this concern as unworthy of the church's mission or the Christian's attention, I would remind the reader that Christ's emphasis upon "love for neighbor" and the biblical teachings of our stewardship of God's gifts should add a Christian dimension to the issue.

We are also reminded in these circumstances of our dependence on one another. I suspect that it is possible to find examples of man's selfishness in times of emergency—we are well aware of the looting that comes in the wake of disasters. I am usually more conscious of the concern and helpfulness that a common emergency produces. Homes are opened, help is offered, communities rally, a sense of oneness is fostered.

But even on a broader base is our dependence in evidence. It becomes more clear that when there is just so much to go around, my usual use may well mean that someone does without. So it is no longer a question of whether or not I can afford it or even can get it. It becomes a moral issue of "loving one's neighbor as one loves himself."

Obviously, we could allow the practices of the out-working of this principle tie us in ethical knots. The difficulty of resolving the problem could easily result in our living by the law of jungle-survival. The end of that route is self-destruction. In saving our lives we will most surely lose them.

Not only is such an attitude self-destructive but it is non-Christian. Love calls us to live our lives in consideration of others. The Bible is very clear that love has the practical dimensions related to the physical needs of persons.

The circumstances that prompted this editorial will no doubt change as the seasons follow each other and spring arrives. The principles that underlie this editorial remain. Grandpa's money will "get all" unless we change our prodigal ways. Our oneness with the human family warrants serious reflection on the fact. Indeed, as Christians we have a more basic reason to examine our lifestyle in light of our call to stewardship and our obligation to love our neighbor even as we love ourselves.

Observations on Parenting

We have Mother's Day and Father's Day on our calendars. We observe Children's Day in some of our churches. Somewhere in all of this there should be Parents' Day—what God has joined let us not put asunder.

Contrary to the prophet Amos' disclaimer, I am both a parent and a son of parents. I make no claim to being an authority nor a model to be followed. But I do have some experience. I also have been an observer of the current scene and have some knowledge of what the Bible says about the subject. With such credentials, let me make some observations. I will limit myself to three.

A healthy marriage is the foundation to good parenting. When there are good vibrations between husband and wife it enhances their role as mother and father. Love between parents creates a sense of security for the children. There is an atmosphere in such a home that children feel and a visitor can sense.

John Drescher, who has written much concerning parenting and family, has pointed out that the best thing a father can do for his children is to love their mother; the best thing the mother can do for her children is to love their father. A healthy marriage is the foundation of a healthy home.

This does not mean that there are no rough places in the marital road nor that parents wear masks to hide their feelings. It does mean that understanding and forgiveness are ingredients of a healthy marriage. It means that trust and love and kindness are in evidence and openly expressed. It means that the marriage is not only held together by faithfulness to the vows but by love for one another.

Of inestimable value in all of this is the model this relationship provides for sons and daughters preparing for and entering into their own marriages. How great the tragedy when two join in the marriage vow having no model either in their parents or their peers for a God-ordained, wholesome marriage. Twice blest is that couple who bring to their own children two models of a happy marriage.

Discipline is not synonymous with punishment. In fact discipline is more nearly synonymous with love.

Somewhere along the line we have come to equate discipline with punishment. To discipline a child is to punish him. At the same time we contrast love and discipline. ("I loved her too much; I just couldn't bring myself to discipline her.")

Discipline may certainly involve punishment. Indeed, punishment may be a necessary part of the resolving of the child's guilt. But discipline is not primarily punishment.

Discipline is the training of a child to do what he or she ought to do. This is in contrast to doing what they want to do or feel like doing. This involves the postponement of present gratification for future satisfaction. It expresses itself in tasks being done and done well, in responsibilities being assumed and carried out, and authority recognized and respected.

Discipline is attained by various means. Clear and consistent directions and expectations are necessary. A parent who calls for certain action but makes no effort to see that the child responds, will soon have no recourse but violence and that with little chance of success. Anyone can give orders. The test of parenting is to see that the child learns to obey.

Discipline involves modeling. Undisciplined parents will hardly produce disciplined children. But parents who are themselves disciplined ethically and emotionally will teach far more by their own actions than by their words. Discipline is a quality of character that creates an atmosphere within the home that fosters disciplined lives in the children.

This discipline is not regimentation nor authoritarian. The individuality of the child needs to be respected. Reasons should be given for the behavior expected. Kindness and understanding are ingredients of love. The expectations which parents have and which they convert to concrete rules in the home need to be matched with affection. Discipline does not mean the breaking of our children's will but rather the molding of that will to do what they ought to do.

Values are the most valuable part of the family inheritance. The lives of our children consist of the choices they make. These choices are determined by the values they hold. These values will be determined by the influences on their lives—influences of home and school, of church and peers. Obviously parents have a crucial role in the transmitting of values.

Parents transmit values by the conscious precept. Much more is transmitted by the unconscious acts and reactions to life. If material values become the usual subject of mealtime conversation, one could expect that these values will seem important to the children. If concern for the needs of others frequently surface in family conversations, children will come to value service and compassion. When the church and the Bible occupy places of importance for the parents and receive their respect and loyalty, one should not find it difficult to understand why the children will give service to the church and obedience to the Word.

A disciplined person with wrong values is a menace to society. High on the parental agenda is the matter of values which are transmitted—transmitted more by life than by word.

None of us receives a 4.0 grade average in the school of parenting. Strength in one area compensates for lack in another. But serious lack in any one portends problems.

Children need that security that comes from a home where the parents are in love and respect each other—who in the best sense of the term have a happy marriage. It is nigh impossible to build a healthy home on a sick marriage.

Children need to learn discipline—to do what they ought rather than what they feel like. The fruit of discipline is not only doing what we ought rather than what we want, but wanting to do what we ought.

Children need Christian values by which to live. They must be saved the trauma which comes when the values they observe in the home are different from those they hear in church. Values may well be the most valuable part of the estate we will pass on as parents. And on it there is no inheritance tax.

The Peril of Relevance

I CORINTHIANS 1:17—2:4

In the first two chapters of First Corinthians Paul goes to some length to emphasize the centrality of the cross in the Christian message. He also shares how in his own ministry he seeks to safeguard this centrality.

His preaching was "not with eloquent wisdom lest the cross be emptied of its power." He did not proclaim the "testimony of God in lofty words of wisdom." He states that he was with them "in weakness and in much fear and trembling and my speech and my message were not plausible [persuasive] words of wisdom."

Paul is saying that he did not try to impress his audience by his logic nor his method. The cross runs counter to human logic, and human charisma tends to detract from the cross.

Let us not use these Scriptures as an excuse for dull and fuzzy preaching. Paul was not making a plea for poor preaching. He was, without doubt, an effective communicator. A dull preacher does not get put in prison although he may be run out of the pulpit. What Paul is calling for is proclamation, whether written or spoken, which by both content and method does not detract from the radical nature of the cross and does not camouflage this central element of the Christian message.

Paul warns of two dangers which are present to those who are zealous: the peril of seeking to be relevant and the temptation to be pragmatic.

The peril of relevance: Paul recognized that to the world the cross is irrelevant—in fact it is foolishness and a stumbling block. The temptation is very real to let our audience set the agenda and we adapt the message to this agenda. This Paul refused to do. The cross which ran counter to the world's wisdom and man's obsession with power is God's agenda.

We may well ask if the emphasis upon Christ providing fulfillment and the resolution of our problems, and supplying happiness and personal peace, adequately represents the radical nature of the cross with its call to repentance and death. The emphasis upon positive thinking and the eternal smile hardly do justice to the cross. We offer Christ as a means to satisfy the world's desire rather than allow the cross to stand in judgment of those desires.

The peril of being pragmatic: Paul was concerned that his method did not hide the cross. One is impressed with the rather low-key nature of his presentation.

One wonders what Paul would say about some of our attempts to capture the public interest and to make the gospel attractive. On how many TV programs do you think he would be a guest speaker or at least be asked for a return appearance. There is something incongruous about using methods of Madison Avenue to promote the message of the Crucified One. One wonders what Hollywood and Golgotha have in common.

As a result, our message and our methods determine the watershed of character rather than the cross becoming this watershed (1:18). I suspect that there are those who would find the cross wisdom and power but who have never really been confronted with the cross. The cross has been hidden behind our sophisticated message and our glamorous methods. I wonder if the opposite may not also be true. There are those who are "in" because they have not really been confronted by the cross. They continue to live by the world's wisdom and power. Like the crowd which followed Jesus for the loaves and fishes, they turn away, finding the cross too hard to bear (John 6).

Paul is asking that the doctrine of the cross, which is prominent in our theology, become clearly evident in our message and determinative of our methods. For it is neither by logic nor cleverness that God's power will be seen. God's power resides in the cross made effective by the Spirit.

We Need a Telescope

Many of us have had the experience of stepping into a room and having our attention taken by a painting hanging on the wall. We are fascinated by it. We change our position, looking at the painting from several vantage points. Now we decide to move closer so that we can see it better. But the nearer we come to the painting the less impressed we are. The details become more prominent but the impact and meaning have been lost. In our effort to see more we see less. Perspective and wholeness have been lost.

I believe that this is a proper analogy to bring to bear upon the current emphasis upon Bible study. We need to bring to our study of the Bible the Bible's perspective and wholeness of view. We have been and continue to concentrate on limited portions of Scripture, attempting to find in these God's word for our need. A portion is too often studied in isolation without the full biblical message being brought to bear upon it. What a person or group may "get out" of this portion may be quite far from the scriptural message. Or the meaning of the portion may for all practical purposes be lost because the wider biblical perspective is not brought to bear upon it.

This does not mean that portions of Scripture should not be studied in depth. It does suggest that leader and student will need to devote time and effort to understand the Bible as a whole. There is need to see the panorama of biblical history and God's actions. We need to understand the mountain peaks of God's revelation as recorded in the Scriptures. We need to understand the various literary forms God used to transmit his revelation and how to interpret this variety of form—poetry for instance is not narrative and should not be interpreted in the same manner as narrative is interpreted. There are biblical themes that run through Scripture like strong strands in a fabric holding the Bible together as a unit. There is the Old Covenant and the New, and between them there is both continuity and discontinuity.

We will not all become Bible scholars, but discipleship calls for us to be Bible students. We all need to seek for that biblical perspective and wholeness which enlightens the smaller portions of the Scriptures. This means that we come to the Bible for more than inspiration; we come for biblical knowledge.

For our biblical perspective we need to provide a theological framework. This framework will give form and consistency to our understanding of the Bible. A theological framework will aid us in maintaining a biblical tension between biblical truths and alert us when these tensions are giving way.

I hear the call from among us for biblical preaching and teaching. This will not happen until we become more serious about biblical knowledge and the entire biblical message. This will not happen until we wrestle with and articulate a theology. Our pulpits will become stronger and our smaller group study sessions will take on meaning if we can recover the wholeness and the grandeur of the biblical message.

We have been using the microscope too much—examining our own feelings, emphasizing our own needs, and focusing on words and phrases from isolated portions of Scripture. What we need is to turn to the telescope. Focus it on God's entire revelation, experience the scope and grandeur of the biblical message and see each portion of Scripture from the biblical perspective. Do not sell your microscope; you will need it on occasion. But the current need is for the longer and the wider view which the telescope provides.

This longer and wider view will bring new dynamic to our preaching. It will add new meaning to our experiences. It will also add significance to those chapters and verses which we will be reading and studying.

A Martyr's Faith

I was standing in the registration line for my first year in seminary when Bob located me. Bob Jacoby was a second-year student at the seminary. We had known each other from our college days together at Franklin and Marshall.

Bob was working with the seminary in the registration and was concerned about a Chinese student who was coming to Princeton for a year of study. So he had come to me to inquire if I would be prepared to share a room with Mr. Koa during the school year. To this I agreed and we shared a room in Alexander Hall.

My Chinese roommate had been a communist. In fact, he had been a rising star in the Communist Party in China. He had been sent to Moscow to study. Upon his return he was ordered to the Philippines to organize the Communist Party there. He returned to China during the days when the Communist party was still illegal and he found himself in prison.

While in prison he came in contact with some Christians and was given a Bible. Through this he became a Christian and later a teacher in a seminary in southeast China. Now he had come to Princeton for additional training prior to assuming the presidency of the seminary.

During the year (1949-50) Mr. Koa was in seminary, the Communists took over China and Chiang Kai-shek and his nationalist government fled to Taiwan. With the Communists now in power, what would Mr. Koa do? He was offered the opportunity to go to the Philippines to minister to the Chinese colony there. But he chose to return to China.

I can only imagine what thoughts went through his mind as he made his decision to return. He was an ex-communist. He was a leader in the Christian church. I am certain that the possibility of imprisonment or even martyrdom was present in his mind as he made the decision to return. This, I believe, is what Jesus was talking about in Luke 9.

When Jesus stated that discipleship involved taking up the cross (Luke 9:23), his hearers heard more than a call to suffering and hardship. They had seen or known of too many crucifixions to see in Jesus' statement anything less than a call to death. Both the imagery and the context (Luke 9:18-27) are evidence that Jesus meant that discipleship calls for a commitment that includes the possibility of death.

This principle of discipleship soon took on significance as Jesus' prediction of his own death was fulfilled and within a generation, according to tradition, all but one of the apostles had been martyred. Martyrdom was to be the lot of many in those early centuries and the centuries since. Faithful disciples died at the hands of the church, the state, and pagan peoples.

Some died because they refused to offer incense at the shrine of the emperor, others because they owned a Bible. For some it was because they refused to have their children baptized as infants; for many it was because they would not deny their faith.

In Luke 9 Jesus calls all his followers to a martyr's faith—not all to a martyr's death, but all to a martyr's faith. It is hard from where we stand to describe a martyr's faith, but we need to attempt to discover what it means to not count our life dear, to take the cross. We need to understand the biblical meaning of saving faith.

It is a faith that seriously counts the cost of following as well as the blessings of receiving. There is indication that the reward of this faith is joy and a great sense of God's presence, but the decision is made in full knowledge that it may be a call to suffering and privation even unto death.

It is a faith that rests upon a decision made at the very center of our being. A faith that goes beyond assent to dogma, the emotions of the moment, and conformity to peer pressure. It is a decision that burns bridges behind and goes forward to the point of no return. Persuaded of the truth of the gospel, won by God's love and the Spirit's power, and convinced that Christ is indeed Lord, we cast our lot with him whatever the cost.

If I would judge the Christian faith by the evangelical books that are being published, it would hardly occur to me that the Christian life is a life that costs everything—that the heroes of our faith were hunted as animals, tortured for their faith, and burned at the stake.

If I would judge the Christain faith by the evangelical radio and television programs, it would never occur to me that the eleventh chapter of Hebrews is the Christian Hall of Fame.

Nor is that Hall of Fame compiled by the writer to the Hebrews complete. For in most centuries since the writer to the Hebrews penned that list, there have been those who have joined them. They lived in the catacombs during the rule of the Caesars; they hid in the mountains of Europe hunted by both catholics and protestants. They fled from country to country in search of sanctuary. *Martyrs Mirror* chronicles those who died during the radical reformation. Fox's *The Book of Martyrs* tells the story of the English martyrs under Queen Mary's persecution.

Korea, China, Indonesia, Vietnam, Uganda, and Russia add to this noble line. Who knows where persecution will come next. One is tempted to ask if what passes among us today for Christian faith bears any resemblance to that of which martyrs are made.

This is not a call for persecution nor a lament that most of us who read these lines know nothing of living in peril for our faith. What I do call for is an understanding that although not all are called to a martyr's death, we are all called by Christ's own words to a martyr's faith. "Whoever does not bear his own cross and come after me, cannot be my disciple" (Luke 14:27).

A Breakthrough by the Spirit

The institution of slavery dates back to the dawn of history. As a spoil of war, servitude was often the lot of the conquered. There are indications that the practice—at least in the West—was in decline until the opening of the continent of Africa and the discovery of

America in the 15th and 16th centuries. A reservoir of black labor in Africa and the need for cheap labor in the colonies of the New World revived the institution of slavery.

It is with slavery in United States that we are most familiar. Until 120 years ago, slavery was legal in the southern states of the United States and the rights of slave owners were recognized by the northern states. Slavery was not a practice engaged in only by those outside the church. Christians were slave holders and the church found and offered justification for the institution of slavery.

Slavery was justified on logical, pragmatic, and biblical grounds. It was necessary for the economic well-being of society. It was assumed that certain peoples were destined to rule, others destined to serve.

The church found Scriptures to justify the practice. The curse upon Canaan (Genesis 9:25-27) was cited in support of slavery. Slavery was practiced by Israel with provisions in the Mosaic code regulating it.

The New Testament writers did not explicitly forbid slavery. Paul gave counsel to both slave and master (Ephesians 6:5-9, et al). He sent the runaway slave Onesimus back to his master, Philemon. Although Paul made some interesting suggestions to Philemon regarding Onesimus, he did not regard his house in Rome as a station of the "underground railroad."

I am not suggesting that any of these Scriptures or all of them together justify the practice of human slavery, or permit Christians to engage in it. What I am pointing out is that Christians, wishing to justify slavery, found Scriptures which they interpreted to support their position.

But the Spirit was not without a witness. Christians such as William Wilberforce in England (1759-1833), John Woolman (1720-1772), and Harriet Beecher Stowe (1811-1896) in the United States began to speak out against this evil. The Quakers and other Christian groups added to the prophetic voice. (Opposition to the holding of slaves by Methodists was one of the principle issues which led to the founding of the Wesleyan Methodist Church in 1843).

Individual voices and awakened churches began to voice the inconsistency of being a follower of Jesus Christ and a holder of slaves. The result was to bring the Christian church to an understanding of the contradiction between the Christian faith and the institution of slavery.

Today the practice of slavery would find no support within the Christian church. A practice that had a long tradition finally came under the judgment of the gospel. This happened as Spirit-led individuals and groups saw the inhumanity and unchristian nature of the practice, and through their witness the truth became clear to the Christian church.

I find it difficult to escape the analogy between the institution of slavery and the practice of war. The Christian church is today with the question of war where the church of 150 years ago was with the question of slavery.

What economic well-being was to slavery, national security is to war. Biblical texts are used to justify the Christian's participation in warfare. The church weighs text against text and comes out in favor of war as their ancestors weighed text against text and came out in support of slavery.

Is it possible that the Christian church, in its justification of war, has subordinated the teaching of Christ to the practices which existed under the Old Covenant—a covenant which the writer to the Hebrews stated is now "obsolete" (Hebrews 8:13 NIV)? Is it possible that when the real test comes Caesar, rather than Christ, is found to be really lord? Is it possible that in the crucial hour of testing, national loyalties would take precedence over love for Christian brethren and sisters, and the state which is transient in nature would take precedence over the church which is supranational and eternal?

I am not suggesting that war would be as easy to outlaw as slavery or even possible to outlaw at all. What I am calling for is that the Christian church and individual Christians witness against this great evil by refusing to participate in its carnage, and that in an act of obedience to Christ we place ourselves on the side of peace, with its unknown possibilities, rather than on the side of war, with the certainty of mass destruction and the incredible cost in human lives and Christian values. If the way of peace is naive, the way of war is surely madness.

Christ promised that the Holy Spirit would lead his church into truth. (John 16:12-15) He suggests that truths not yet understood by his disciples would become clear under the ministry of the Spirit.

I would like to believe that we may be at a crucial time in the life of the church when the Spirit is seeking to "guide the followers of Christ into all truth." Using those whose conscience against war has been sensitized, the Spirit will lead this generation of Christians to see the demonic nature of war as our fathers were led to see the demonic nature of slavery.

Are we as Christians prepared to renounce the empty promises of power and to commit ourselves to the costly but hopeful alternative of love, reaffirming our faith in the cross and the resurrection?

A Sobering Truth

Life is too short, and eternity is too long, to live or to die with an unforgiving spirit.

It is commonly accepted among us that man stands in need of God's forgiveness. What is not as commonly understood is that God's forgiveness is directly related to our forgiveness of our fellowmen.

"For if you forgive men when they sin against you, your heavenly Father will also forgive you. But if you do not forgive men their sins, your Father will not forgive your sins" (Matthew 6:14, 15).

"And when you stand praying, if you hold anything against anyone, forgive him, so that your Father in heaven may forgive you your sins" (Mark 11:25).

(The Parable of the Unmerciful Servant). In anger his master turned him over to the jailers until he should pay back all he owed.

"This is how my heavenly Father will treat each of you unless you forgive your brother from your heart" (Matthew 18:34, 35).

In the Ephesian letter Paul calls upon the reader to,

"Get rid of all biterness, rage and anger, brawling and slander, along with every form of malice. Be kind and compassionate to one another, just as in Christ God forgave you" (4:31, 32).

In Paul's letter to the Galatians he includes along with the sins of immorality ". . . hatred, discord, . . . dissensions, factions . . ." and then adds, "I warn you, as I did before, that those who live like this will not inherit the kingdom of God" (5:20, 21).

Permit me to make five observations:

An unforgiving spirit nullifies God's forgiving grace. This may run counter to our theology, but the statements of Jesus are so forthright that I am compelled to include them in my understanding of salvation.

We misread the meaning of God's grace when we presume that God's forgiveness is effective regardless of our response. We fail to understand the offer of God's forgiveness when, like the unforgiving servant, we have been forgiven so much yet withhold our forgiveness for much lesser offenses.

Forgiveness is costly. It should not be assumed that it is ever easy. The cross should be evidence of this. In the midst of that cosmic event Jesus spoke the word of forgiveness even as he paid the price of ours.

So we should not assume that we can really deal with hurts and offenses by simply saying "That's O.K." or "Just forget it." Granting forgiveness may well take a dying to pride and to self. It will call for prayer and divine aid. Forgiveness is a product of God's grace; a fruit of the Spirit. Hatred and revenge are the world's way of dealing with hurts and offenses. These are in Satan's game plan. How we respond is evidence of whose children we are—children of God or children of the world.

A **forgiving** spirit is an essential and unique quality of life within the church. It is really what the church is all about—a forgiven and forgiving community.

Jesus revealed the importance of a forgiving spirit within the church when he outlined a pattern of dealing with offenses between members. It is essential to forgive with my heart the one who has wronged me, even if forgiveness is not sought (e.g. Stephen and Jesus). But I need to do more. I need to seek to restore the broken relationship that has occurred between me and the other person.

The witness of a church is clearly affected—for good or ill—by the life of its members. The ministry of the church is hindered by sin within the body. I would venture that an unforgiving spirit—resentments held and hurts nurtured—does more to destroy the church's witness and hinder its ministry than the moral and ethical sins which are usually thought of when we speak of sin within the church.

The principle that the sins of the parents are visited upon the children is nowhere more evident that in the case of an unforgiving spirit. For the sake of the children parents cannot afford to harbor resentment and ill-will. It tends to nullify whatever Christian nurture is attempted by parents or church. It embitters the children towards the church and the Christian faith.

I have seen families lost to the church and to the kingdom because a father was unwilling to forgive or a mother nurtured a hurt which grew until, like a cancer, it permeated her life. Indeed the personalities of children are often warped and poisoned by the bitterness reflected in the home.

Life is too short and eternity is too long to live or to die with an unforgiving spirit.

We do not minimize the effect that an unforgiving spirit has on the person who harbors it, nor the devastating effect it has on the children who grow up in an atmosphere of bitterness and resentment, nor the effect this has on the life and witness and ministry of the church, nor what it does to relationships on the job or in the community. But the most sobering fact is that the Bible offers little or no eternal hope for one who harbors an unforgiving spirit. He or she remains unforgiven by God.

The Bible clearly teaches that it is God's forgiveness that provides an alternative to his judgment. When we close the channels to God's forgiveness we come under his judgment.

Let us not presume on God's grace by assuming that Christ really did not mean what he so clearly said, "For if ye do not forgive men their sins, your heavenly Father will not forgive your sins."

It bears repeating—life is too short and eternity is too long to live or to die with an unforgiving spirit.

On the Reading of Church Bulletins

A sizeable number of church bulletins come to my desk. It is just possible that the number may decrease following this editorial.

I do read these bulletins. It is an interesting experience. Church bulletins will never be found in an anthology of great literature but they do reflect the character and life of a congregation and, like letters, say something about the times and the writers.

This editorial is no attempt at profundity, but I use it as an opportunity to share observations made after more than ten years of reading church bulletins.

Observation 1: One of the most important investments a congregation can make is the purchase of a good typewriter and a good duplicating machine, or the contracting for the services of such equipment. High among congregational gifts is that of typists and duplicator operators.

For many congregations the church bulletin is the closest they come to the publishing of promotional material. If the bulletin is poorly printed, the copy poorly arranged, and errors abounding, the devil can breathe a little easier.

I used to think that the "church bulletin humor," which appeared in the *Reader's Digest* and similar publications, was contrived. I no longer am so skeptical. It is a sense of brotherhood which restrains me from printing a similar, occasional column in the *Visitor*.

Observation 2: I often note the absence of a sermon title. My initial and involuntary reaction is "Why no title?" The most charitable explanation is that the bulletin was prepared and printed early in the week. The sermon had not yet been named.

Sometimes charity does not prevail and I am tempted to wonder if the absence of a sermon title is indicative of the low priority in time and importance given to this part of the worship service. So instead of assuming that the bulletin was printed too early I am tempted to assume that the sermon was prepared too late.

Observation 3: I am impressed with the number of "special programs" which are included in the congregation's life. I define "special programs" as those which do not use the resources of the staff and local membership but are built upon guest speakers, films, artists, or groups.

Along with my observation, however, I do have some real concerns. We need to constantly ask if we are confusing entertainment with worship and emphasizing inspiration at the cost of a word from God.

Malcolm Muggeridge has raised serious questions concerning the ability of the television medium to communicate the gospel. He has no doubt overstated his case. But he has brought to the front the relation of the medium to the message. At what point does the integrity of the gospel message suffer and even get lost in the search for a method which entertains?

Another concern relates to what a constant and extensive use of resources from outside our congregation does to us. The programs and public services of a congregation call for purpose—not just the filling of a schedule. With that in mind, judgment needs to be exercised in the selection of "special events."

To open our pulpits to those of another doctrinal tradition can easily be interpreted by the congregation as support of that tradition. It is not so much what is said in the pulpit as the imprimatur which the opening of the pulpit gives to that tradition.

A similar situation develops when opportunity is given to an organization. Often their presentation is more obviously promotional than the doctrinal position of a guest speaker may be. This has a tendency to divert funds, loyalty, and personnel to ministries which are no more worthy and sometimes less worthy of our support than we are our own programs.

I am neither suggesting the closing of our pulpits to outside speakers nor our Sunday evening hours to special programs. This would be neither wise nor practical.

The concern is that pastors and church boards and program planners be aware of the influence which these special programs have on the life and future of the congregation. Programs should have purpose beyond the filling of an hour on Sunday evening or doing something "special" on a Sunday morning.

The purpose of our public services is well summarized in Ephesians 4:12:

> "For the equipment of the saints for the work of the ministry, for building up the body of Christ, until we all attain to the unity of the faith and of the knowledge of the Son of God, to mature manhood, to the measure of the stature of the fulness of Christ, so that we may no longer be children, tossed to and fro and carried about with every wind of doctrine . . ."

It would be well to read our church bulletins in light of that purpose.